JESUS IN THE GOSPELS

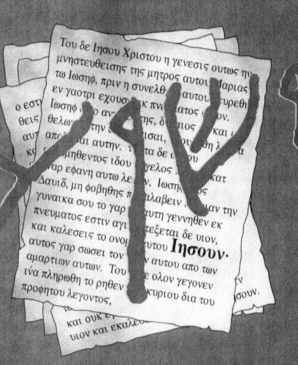

Leader Guide

DISCIPLE
Second Generation Studies

JESUS IN THE GOSPELS
DISCIPLE Second Generation Studies
Leader Guide

Scripture quotations in this publication are from the New Revised Standard Version of the Bible,
copyright © 1989 by the Division of Christian Education of the National Council of the Churches
of Christ in the United States of America. Used by permission. All rights reserved.

The Hebraica (R) and Graeca (R) fonts used to print this work are available from
Linguist's Software, Inc., PO Box 580, Edmonds, WA 98020-0580 USA tel (206) 775-1130.

Nellie M. Moser, Senior Editor; Mark Price, Development Editor; Amy Cain, Production Editor;
Linda O. Spicer, Unit Assistant; Ed Wynne, Production & Design Manager.

For more information about JESUS IN THE GOSPELS training seminars or DISCIPLE training seminars,
call toll free 800-251-8591 or 800-672-1789
fax 615-749-6049
www.cokesbury.com/services/secondgeneration.asp

03 04 05 06 07 08 09 10 11 12 — 10 9 8 7 6 5 4 3 2 1

Contents

A Word About This Study

JESUS IN THE GOSPELS focuses on the portraits of Jesus found in the four Gospels—Matthew, Mark, Luke, and John. The word *in* used in the title signals that this study takes an approach different from the familiar "life and teaching of Jesus" approach of reading stories and accounts of what Jesus said and did in order to draw conclusions about their meaning and about who Jesus was. *This study looks at the way each Gospel writer presents events and teachings and at the picture of Jesus that emerges in each of the Gospels.*

To know who Jesus is, we must study the Jesus in the Gospels. The four canonical portraits—the heart of this study—focus on Jesus himself by the ways they situate him in time and place. The history-rooted Jesus in the Gospels challenges preconceived ideas about Jesus. For those who think of Jesus as merely an intriguing figure from the past, the historical and canonical portraits of Jesus will show them the Jesus who is more than a figure to be memorialized.

Each Gospel has a distinctive angle of vision. Most readers of Scripture tend to read the Gospels and put the stories together into one story—one Jesus. But that one Jesus is not the church's Jesus. The church has never substituted a single story for the Jesus of the four Gospels. Each Gospel's way of presenting Jesus and his significance reflects not just the writer's view of Jesus and events but also reflects what was going on in the writer's church. These differences in perspective on Jesus provide opportunities to understand and appropriate more than one way of following Jesus.

Reading is not passive. Many DISCIPLE graduates who come to this study will have studied the life and teaching of Jesus or the life and ministry of Jesus, but few will ever have studied Jesus in the various ways the Gospels present him. This approach to study of the Gospels requires and involves the participant in close reading of the text. The Bible discloses its meanings to those who stay with it long enough to get something out of it.

Think of preparation in terms of commitment not convenience. JESUS IN THE GOSPELS takes critical scholarship seriously and therefore requires of participants skill in comparing and analyzing various Gospel passages, and biblical knowledge that enables participants to place particular New Testament passages about Jesus in their Old Testament context. In other words, participant preparation is rigorous.

DISCIPLE graduates will recognize that an increased amount of time is required for daily study because of the detailed reading called for in daily assignments. Completing daily assignments will involve use of the Bible, the study manual, and Gospel Comparisons.

Bring appropriate expectations to this study. What may participants expect of this study? Participants may expect to gain a fuller understanding of and appreciation for the four Gospels as richly textured portraits of Jesus.

Participants may expect to see the varying portraits of Jesus as opportunities to understand and appropriate more than one way of following Jesus.

Participants may expect to gain appreciation for Jesus; for the complexity of Jesus' historical time and place; and, in particular, for his Jewishness.

Participants may expect to be confronted weekly by Jesus and summoned to deeper allegiance and loyalty to Jesus.

Participants may expect that this study of Jesus, while taking critical scholarship seriously, will enrich rather than impoverish their understanding of Jesus.

Participants may expect to understand what is at stake in doctrinal claims about Jesus that have roots in Scripture.

Participants may expect to converse more seriously than in the past about their Christian heritage in Jesus, to be able to take a stand—this is what we believe.

Participants may expect to continually confront the question, What constitutes my followship?

In terms of approach to study, participants may expect daily disciplined reading and study of Scripture with growing attention to detail.

Participants may expect regularly to use their Bible, their study manual, and their Gospel Comparisons together in daily study.

Participants may expect to learn anew that the Old Testament permeates the whole Bible, that the Gospel writers and Jesus relied on the Old Testament; it was their Scripture, the only Scripture they knew.

Participants may expect to be surprised, to be shocked, to be made uncomfortable, to be stretched, to be awed, to be comforted, and to experience hope and peace.

The Study Manual

The study manual guides daily study and preparation for the weekly group session. All lessons have the same elements each designated by a scriptural phrase. While these main elements always appear in the same sequence in each lesson, they function like the interwoven strands of a web. This function reflects the rhythm of the study that involves moving back and forth among the Bible, the study manual, and the Gospel Comparisons.

The Format

- The lesson title and printed Scripture that follows indicate the lesson's focus. The lesson title serves also as the heading for the commentary portion of the lesson in the study manual.
- *"They Have No Wine"* is the heading for a brief statement about some aspect of the human condition that is addressed, sometimes indirectly, by the week's study. It intends to be suggestive, to alert the reader to some part of daily life that needs attention.
- *"Beginning With Moses and All the Prophets"* is the heading for the reading assignments and suggestions of things to look for during each day's study. The scriptural phrase signals that to understand Jesus in the Gospels requires attending also to the Old Testament.
- *"Do You Want to Become His Disciples, Too?"* is the heading for the response section of the study manual. The paragraphs here are designed to stimulate thoughtful reflection about the discipleship Jesus calls for. This section always includes a question or a suggestion inviting a written response as a starting point for discussing the Jesus in the week's Scriptures.
- The prayers printed in the study manual at the end of each lesson all come from the Psalms and are quoted from The Contemporary English Version. The psalm can be a starting point for participants to use in composing their own prayers each day and is used to conclude the group session each week.

The "So Then" section of the lesson commentary highlights information, ideas, and perspectives presented in the lesson and helps the reader begin to see connections between the biblical passages studied and their lives. Each week, through "So Then," readers will come to understand how the biblical material challenges the way they think or act and how the perspectives of the Gospel writers connect with, inform, and inspire their own perspectives.

Although this section varies in length according to the lesson content, it generally functions as a summary of the emphases and teachings in the lesson. Sometimes "So Then" draws together insights from more than one lesson because the information needs to be seen as a whole to be thoroughly understood. Sometimes this section will simply restate the main points in the lesson; other times it invites questions, stimulates curiosity, challenges readers' thinking, or draws implications for their lives.

Reading thoroughly "A Word to the Reader" on study manual pages 6–7 *before* beginning the study is an important first step for leaders and group members alike. Information on those pages should be discussed as part of every group's orientation.

Things to Look For

Accompanying each day's Scripture reading assignments are suggestions of things to look for that will take persons deeper into Scripture. The words *note*, *notice*, and *observe* are used often in the suggestions to encourage close attention to detail. One way to think about these three words is to start with the word *see* in the sense of look or use your eyes. *Note*, *notice*, and *observe* all imply using the senses, taking in everything the words you are reading have to deliver. And bringing both curiosity and imagination to the acts of noticing, noting, observing will result in new insights. To *notice* is to give attention, even respectful attention, to the Scripture being read. *Note* implies a careful and deliberate getting in mind what is being seen and read. Couple with that idea another definition of *note*—to write down or make note of. That action goes along with *note* in the sense of seeing or observing. To *observe* is to be aware, to look attentively, to direct one's attention, to detect what is there in the words being read.

One way to fill *note*, *notice*, and *observe* with meaning is to look at some examples of how the words are used in Scripture. Think of all the different ways of understanding what the word is saying in each passage. For example, consider these verses: "And the Lord took *note* of Hannah" (1 Samuel 2:21); "Take *note*, I have told you beforehand"

(Matthew 24:25); "God looked upon the Israelites, and God took *notice* of them" (Exodus 2:25); "Why do you see the speck in your neighbor's eye, but do not *notice* the log in your own eye?" (Luke 6:41); "Look at the heavens and see; *observe* the clouds, which are higher than you" (Job 35:5); "Brothers and sisters, join in imitating me, and *observe* those who live according to the example you have in us" (Philippians 3:17). For every biblical passage you read, *note, notice, observe* it as though you had not seen it before.

Suggestions of things to look for sometimes amount to two or three sentences; other times, several sentences. As the study progresses, the suggestions increase in length and detail thereby developing and sharpening persons' ability to read carefully. The study manual provides space for recording insights, observations, and questions related to the Scripture. This approach to study of the Gospels requires and involves close reading of the text—not to be done on the run, in bits and pieces, or at the last minute.

A helpful sequence of steps for completing daily assignments and working with the suggestions of things to look for appears in a yellow-tinted block on study manual page 7.

Gospel Comparisons

Gospel Comparisons is a companion to the study manual. It contains selected Gospel portions from the New Revised Standard Version printed in multicolumn format to facilitate the comparing of similarities and differences in Gospel accounts of an event, teaching, or story. The printed selections follow the sequence of Scripture treated in the study manual.

GC 1-1 is an example of the symbol that appears in the study manual at the point in any lesson where the Gospel Comparisons is to be used during daily study. (GC means Gospel Comparisons. The first number indicates the lesson and the second number, the Gospel portion to be used at that point in the lesson.) The symbol may appear one or more times in a lesson. A few lessons do not call for use of Gospel Comparisons during daily study. Brief instructions accompany each Gospel portion.

Some Gospel portions are included for use during weekly group study and therefore are not referred to in the study manual. References to their use appear in the leader guide. (For complete information about using Gospel Comparisons, see Gospel Comparisons pages 4–7.)

Biblical References

Bible studies indicate biblical references in various ways. The following examples indicate how the biblical references in this study are to be understood:

Chapter and verse

Matthew 1:1-2 means read Matthew Chapter 1, Verses 1 through 2.
Matthew 1:1-2, 4, 6-8 means read Matthew Chapter 1, Verses 1 through 2, Verse 4, and Verses 6 through 8.

A hyphen is used between verses in sequence as in Matthew 1:1-2.

Commas within a reference separate verses within the same chapter as in Matthew 1:1-2, 4, 6-8.

A semicolon indicates a change of chapter or a change of book as in Malachi 3:1-5; 4; Mark 1:1-8; 6:7-29.

Chapters through chapters

Matthew 1–2 means read the first verse of Chapter 1 through the last verse of Chapter 2.

A dash is used between chapters as in Matthew 1–2 and a hyphen is used between verses as in Matthew 1:1-2.

Portions of more than one chapter within a book

Matthew 1:1–4:4 means begin reading at Matthew Chapter 1, Verse 1 and read all the way through Chapter 4, Verse 4.

Portions spanning two books

2 Chronicles 36:22-23–Ezra 1:1-4 means read 2 Chronicles Chapter 36, Verses 22 through 23 (which ends the book) through Ezra Chapter 1, Verses 1 through 4 (which begins the next book).

Sometimes biblical references within the lesson commentary include the name of the book as well as numbers indicating chapter and verse and sometimes only chapter and verse numbers. The first reference to a particular book lists the name of the book and chapter and verse numbers. If several references to that same book follow, only chapters and verses are listed, not the book name. When a reference is to a different book then the book name is included. When you come across a reference without the name of the book, you can trace the references back to the first mention of the book to know if you're reading in the right book.

The Weekly Group Process

Guidance for each of the thirty group sessions in JESUS IN THE GOSPELS follows a process suggested by the format of the study manual. Each session is designed to take two and one-half hours.

"Coming Together"

The first half hour serves as an entrance into group study and includes prayer, hymn singing, viewing Part I of the video segment, and discussion after viewing. This portion of the weekly session provides the transition between individual preparation and group study.

"Beginning With Moses and All the Prophets" and Study Manual Commentary

The next one and one-half hours concentrate on two related sets of group activities, one dealing primarily with the suggestions of things to look for in the daily assignments and the other dealing with the commentary section in the study manual. The two headings in the leader guide designating these activities carry the same titles as the two corresponding sections in the study manual. It will become apparent early in the study that the preparation group members do each week with the things to look for and the commentary are interconnected and not easily dealt with apart from each other. For this reason the flow of the weekly group session will move back and forth between working with the things to look for and working with the commentary section. Similarly, in this block of time, group members will move back and forth among the Bible, study manual, and Gospel Comparisons.

"Do You Want to Become His Disciples, Too?"

The next twenty-minute portion in each weekly session focuses on persons' responses to their study during the week. Group members hear one another's responses to the question in italics under this section in the study manual. The point of this portion of the weekly session is to describe the Jesus who emerges from the week's Scripture.

"Going Forth"

The final ten minutes of the weekly session is designed to allow for transition in two ways. First, the group shifts focus from their own study to the needs and concerns of others through prayer. Second, by viewing Part II of the week's video, the group shifts, from talking about Jesus to reflecting on Jesus, from examination to celebration. The guidance in the leader guide for this section presumes no discussion will follow the viewing of Part II of the video. Maintaining the intention of this closing portion of the session means hearing prayer concerns, making any necessary announcements, and previewing the next week's lesson *before* viewing Part II of the video.

Points to Keep in Mind

(1) This study uses hymns of Jesus to open each weekly session. The leader guide suggests two hymns, each emphasizing something about the Jesus encountered in the week's study. Have hymnals available for the group to use. If you choose a hymn other than the two suggested, be sure the hymn relates to the Scriptures about Jesus read that week.

(2) A regular break is not scheduled in the leader guide plan for each weekly session. When deciding when to schedule a break, take into account the ninety-minute portion of the weekly meeting may not always be divided equally (forty-five minutes each) between the group activities related to "Beginning With Moses and All the Prophets" and to the study manual commentary. In general, a natural break occurs between those two sets of activities regardless of the time allotments.

(3) The leader guide plan for each session uses small black boxes in the left-hand margins to signal a change in group activity or discussion emphasis. The order of the group activities and discussion questions follows an intentional sequence. The expectation is that the leader guides the group through all the activities and discussion questions written for each session in the leader guide.

(4) The video component comes in VHS and DVD format. If using the VHS, cue Part I of each week's video segment. After viewing Part I at the start of the weekly session stop the tape as soon as possible. Then the tape will be ready for viewing Part II at the close of the session—no cuing is necessary. If using the DVD, with a set-top DVD player, no cuing is necessary. Simply insert Disk 1 or Disk 2, and the main menu screen appears after the copyright notice. Use the *up* or *down* arrow keys on the DVD player or remote to highlight the item to be viewed. A brown arrow appears to the left of the menu item when it is highlighted. Press *play* to view the segment. (Session 30 only has Part II.)

The Videos

The videos for this study are unique and integral to each lesson and weekly group session. The video segment for each lesson has two parts. Part I is a seven-to-ten-minute presentation by a Bible scholar or theologian on some topic or aspect of the subject treated in the lesson. It *begins* the session and is followed by discussion in small groups. The purpose of Part I of each video segment is to enrich learning by taking viewers beyond their own reading and study.

Part II of each video segment brings forward through art, music, words, and movement the Jesus in the week's Scripture. This one-to-three-minute portion of the video *closes* each weekly session; no discussion follows. The purpose of Part II of the video segment absorbs the point of the lesson and celebrates it. Together, the two parts of the video segments are designed to clarify and highlight the distinctive angle of vision from which each Gospel presents Jesus.

A Word About the Art

Every video segment opens with music and a montage of art. Included in the art are the four traditional images depicting the Gospel writers, or Evangelists. The images derive from Ezekiel 1:10 and Revelation 4:7—a winged man (Matthew), a winged lion (Mark), a winged ox (Luke), and an eagle (John). The art of the four images is based on the *Book of Kells*, an illuminated Latin manuscript of the four Gospel texts, produced during the early Middle Ages.

Following the images of the Evangelists, the opening art features a variety of images of Jesus appearing in the four diamond-shaped boxes. One set of eight portraits of Jesus appears in the opening of even-numbered segments and a different set of eight appears in the opening of odd-numbered segments. These sixteen images of Jesus along with scores of other images of Jesus and scenes from the Gospels appearing throughout the videos represent a broad range of artistic expression.

Just as we encounter Jesus in the Gospels portrayed from the perspectives of different writers, we encounter Jesus in the art of the videos from the perspectives of different artists. The selection of art follows the intent of the study: that we are looking for the Jesus *in* the Gospels, rather than the historian's Jesus *behind* the Gospels.

Because the Gospels are proclamation not neutral reporting, they present little in the way of biographical detail or physical descriptions related to Jesus. As a result, artists have sought to portray Jesus in terms of their own time and culture, and through various artistic styles. The colorful Jesus serving as the backdrop to all the video openings reflects the heritage of contemporary Chinese artist He Qi. In contrast, the faces of Jesus painted by Rembrandt reflect the world of seventeenth-century Europe.

In order to fully appreciate the scope of the art in the videos, take time to scan the list of credits at the end of the video summary sheets found inside the VHS or the DVD case. Keep in mind that the expectation of this study is that the many ways Jesus is depicted through art will enhance the many ways Jesus is depicted in the Gospels, and vice versa. This rich complement of study and art will inform the way we see—and follow—Jesus in our own time and place.

A Word About the Music

Much of the music accompanying the video segments comes from the church's hymnody. Hymns telling the story of Jesus are suggested to be sung or read at the beginning of each weekly session. In the same way each video segment uses hymns about Jesus to provide the underscore for selected images and words of Jesus. As you study the story of Jesus week by week, listen for the story to unfold through the music in the videos.

A Word About the Set

The video set design is both a backdrop for the presenters and a visual reminder that the Gospels situate Jesus in time and place. The Galilee of Herod is the Galilee of Jesus, and the Jerusalem of the Temple is the Jerusalem of Jesus. To that end, the set features several "scenes" suggestive of the Palestine Jesus would have known: the doorway of a simple home, a market area, a view of the Sea of Galilee, and a portion of the Temple.

As you listen to the video presentations each week, view the scenes in which they are set as cues to the imagination. In your mind's eye, locate Jesus teaching by the Galilean shore, or coming to the door of the home of Mary and Martha, or talking to a woman by a well, or standing with some Pharisees in the shadow of a Temple column. Be alert to the possibility that what you see will inform what you hear.

Video Presenters

Each JESUS IN THE GOSPELS video segment has two parts (except Segment 30, which has one):
Part I—a presentation by a scholar on some aspect of the lesson's topic, to be viewed at the beginning of the session.
Part II—art, words, and music focusing on the Jesus in the week's Scripture; to be viewed at the closing of the session.

Host: Dr. Priscilla Pope-Levison—Professor of Theology, Seattle Pacific University. A United Methodist clergywoman, Dr. Pope-Levison was formerly on the faculty at North Park Theological Seminary and Duke University Divinity School. She is co-author of *Jesus in Global Contexts*.

Segment 1: Dr. Leander E. Keck—Retired Dean of Yale University Divinity School. Dr. Keck served as Convener of the Editorial Board and Senior New Testament Editor of *The New Interpreter's Bible*. A clergy member of the United Church of Christ, he is author of *Who Is Jesus?* and is currently writing the commentary on Romans for the Abingdon New Testament Commentaries series. He wrote the study manual for JESUS IN THE GOSPELS.

Segment 2: Dr. Dale C. Allison, Jr.—Errett M. Grable Professor of New Testament and Christian Origins, Pittsburgh Theological Seminary. Dr. Allison is author of a dozen books, including *The New Moses: A Matthean Typology* and *The Sermon on the Mount: Inspiring the Moral Imagination*. He is a member of the Presbyterian Church (U.S.A.).

Segment 3: Dr. Sarah J. Tanzer—Professor of New Testament and Early Judaism, McCormick Theological Seminary. Much of her published research focuses on the Gospel of John, wisdom and apocalypticism, early Jewish-Christian relations, and feminist readings of early Jewish and Christian texts. Tanzer, a Jewish scholar, has been a member of the international team responsible for publishing the first edition of two Dead Sea Scroll manuscripts.

Segment 4: Dr. Amy-Jill Levine—E. Rhodes and Leona B. Carpenter Professor of New Testament Studies, Vanderbilt University Divinity School. A member of the Jewish Conservative movement (Orthodox), Dr. Levine is editor of the twelve-volume series *Feminist Companion to the New Testament and Early Christian Literature* and is a lecturer in The Teaching Company's Great Courses series.

Segment 5: Dr. Susan R. Garrett—Professor of New Testament, Louisville Presbyterian Theological Seminary. Dr. Garrett also taught at Candler School of Theology and Yale University Divinity School. A member of the Presbyterian Church (U.S.A.), she is author of *The Temptations of Jesus in Mark's Gospel* and co-author of *Making Time for God: Daily Devotions for Children and Families to Share*.

Segment 6: Dr. Paul N. Anderson—Professor of Biblical and Quaker Studies, George Fox University. Dr. Anderson is a member of the Society of Friends. He is author of *The Christology of the Fourth Gospel: Its Unity and Disunity in the Light of John 6* and is known for his interdisciplinary approach to biblical studies.

Segment 7: Dr. Bruce Chilton—Bernard Iddings Bell Professor of Religion, Bard College, and chaplain of the college. An Episcopal priest, Dr. Chilton is rector of the Free Church of St. John the Evangelist in Barrytown, New York, and Executive Director of the Institute of Advanced Theology. He is author of *Rabbi Jesus: An Intimate Biography*.

Segment 8: Dr. Mark Allan Powell—Professor of New Testament, Trinity Lutheran Seminary. Dr. Powell served as chair of both the Matthew Group and the Historical Jesus Section of the Society of Biblical Literature. He is author of seventeen books, including *Jesus as a Figure in History*, and is a member of the Evangelical Lutheran Church in America.

Segment 9: Dr. Pamela M. Eisenbaum—Associate Professor of Biblical Studies and Christian Origins, Iliff School of Theology. Known for her expertise in Judaism and Christian origins, ancient Jewish-Christian relations, and Pauline studies, Dr. Eisenbaum is one of a growing number of Jewish scholars teaching in Christian seminaries. She is author of *The Jewish Heroes of Christian History: Hebrews 11 in Literary Context* and a contributor to the *Women's Bible Commentary Expanded Edition*.

Segment 10: Dr. Deborah Krause—Associate Professor of New Testament, Eden Theological

Seminary. Dr. Krause's studies specialize in the Gospels and biblical hermeneutics. She is author of *1 Timothy Readings: A New Biblical Commentary*. As a clergy member of the Presbyterian Church (U.S.A.), she serves the church through social justice advocacy, teaching, preaching, and scholarship.

Segment 11: Dr. Michael J. Brown—Assistant Professor of New Testament, Candler School of Theology, Emory University. Dr. Brown is a clergy member of the African Methodist Episcopal Church with interests in Pauline theology, early Christian biblical interpretation, and early North African Christianity. He is author of *What They Don't Tell You: A Survivor's Guide to Academic Biblical Studies* and is currently writing a commentary on the Lord's Prayer.

Segment 12: The Reverend Hyesung Hong Lee—Adjunct Faculty in New Testament, Garrett-Evangelical Theological Seminary. A United Methodist, the Reverend Hong Lee is pastor of Kaneville United Methodist Church in the Northern Illinois Conference. She is Executive Director of the Committee on Korea Reunification and Reconciliation of the National Association of Korean American United Methodist Churches in the U.S.A.

Segment 13: Dr. Beverly R. Gaventa—Professor of New Testament, Princeton Theological Seminary. A member of the Presbyterian Church, Dr. Gaventa is co-editor of *Blessed One: Protestant Perspectives on Mary* and author of *Mary: Glimpses of the Mother of Jesus* and *The Acts of the Apostles* in the Abingdon New Testament Commentaries series. Her specialties within the field of New Testament studies are the letters of Paul and Luke-Acts.

Segment 14: Dr. Emerson B. Powery—Associate Professor of New Testament and Chair of the Department of Theology, Lee University. Dr. Powery is author of *Jesus Reads Scripture* and co-editor of *The Spirit and the Mind: Essays in Informed Pentecostalism*. He is a member of the Church of God.

Segment 15: Dr. Frank Gulley, Jr.—Professor Emeritus of Church History, Vanderbilt University Divinity School. Dr. Gulley is an ordained elder in The United Methodist Church.

Segment 16: Dr. Justo L. González—Retired ministerial member of the Rio Grande Conference of The United Methodist Church. Born in Cuba, Dr. González has devoted most of his career to theological education and writing. He is author of

over fifty books, including *Three Months with Matthew*, and co-author of the commentary on the book of Revelation in the Westminster Bible Companion series.

Segment 17: Dr. Dan P. Cole—Professor Emeritus of Religion and Mediterranean Archaeology, Lake Forest College. A United Methodist minister, Dr. Cole spent one decade in congregational ministry followed by four decades of college teaching in biblical studies and archaeology. For sixteen seasons Cole participated in archaeological excavations in Jordan and Israel.

Segment 18: Dr. John R. Levison—Professor of New Testament, Seattle Pacific University. Dr. Levison was Honorary Visiting Lecturer at the University of St. Andrews in Scotland, Alexander von Humboldt Fellow at the University of Tubingen in Germany, and Fellow at the National Humanities Center. A United Methodist, he is co-author of *Jesus in Global Contexts*.

Segment 19: Dr. Osvaldo D. Vena—Associate Professor of New Testament Interpretation, Garrett-Evangelical Theological Seminary. Dr. Vena has published articles in English and Spanish and is author of *The Parousia and Its Rereadings: The Development of the Eschatological Consciousness in the New Testament Writings*. He is an ordained minister of the Reformed Church of Argentina.

Segment 20: Dr. L. Gregory Jones—Dean and Professor of Theology, Duke University Divinity School. Dr. Jones is author or editor of twelve books. He and his wife are both ministerial members of the Western North Carolina Conference of The United Methodist Church; together they wrote *Mending Lives: The Power of Forgiveness in Christian Life and Faith*.

Segment 21: Dr. Peter J. Storey—Professor of the Practice of Christian Ministry, Duke University Divinity School. Dr. Storey is a widely traveled preacher, a former bishop in the Methodist Church of Southern Africa, and was one of the church leaders engaged in the anti-apartheid struggles in South Africa.

Segment 22: Dr. Ellen T. Charry—Associate Professor of Systematic Theology, Princeton Theological Seminary. Dr. Charry is author of *Inquiring After God: Classic and Contemporary Readings* and *By the Renewing of Your Minds: Pastoral Function of Christian Doctrine*. She has served as editor of *Theology Today* and as editor-at-large for *The Christian Century*. She is a member of the Episcopal church.

Segment 23: Dr. Gail R. O'Day—A. H. Shatford Professor of New Testament and Preaching, Candler School of Theology, Emory University. A member of the United Church of Christ, Dr. O'Day is co-editor of *The Oxford Access Bible* and a contributor to *The New Interpreter's Bible*. She is author of *The Word Disclosed: Preaching the Gospel of John*.

Segment 24: Dr. R. Alan Culpepper—Founding Dean of the McAfee School of Theology, Mercer University. A Southern Baptist and son of missionaries to Chile and Argentina, he taught at Southern Baptist Theological Seminary in Louisville and at Baylor University. He is the author of *The Gospel and Letters of John* in the Abingdon Interpreting Biblical Texts series.

Segment 25: Dr. Jaime Clark-Soles—Assistant Professor of New Testament, Perkins School of Theology, Southern Methodist University. Dr. Clark-Soles is author of *Scripture Cannot Be Broken: The Social Function of the Use of Scripture in the Fourth Gospel*. An American Baptist minister, she has served in local church and hospice settings. Her special interests include the use of Scripture among sectarian groups, ancient views of death and afterlife, and forgiveness in the New Testament.

Segment 26: Dr. Robert D. Kysar—Bandy Professor Emeritus of Preaching and New Testament, Candler School of Theology, Emory University. Dr. Kysar has taught both preaching and New Testament in Lutheran and United Methodist seminaries. A clergy member of the Evangelical Lutheran Church in America, he is author of eighteen books, including *Preaching John*.

Segment 27: Dr. Carolyn A. Osiek—Professor of New Testament, Catholic Theological Union. A Roman Catholic sister, R.S.C.J., Dr. Osiek is a frequent director of biblical travel and study programs. She is co-author of *Families in the New Testament World: Households and House Churches* and former president of the Catholic Biblical Association of America.

Segment 28: Dr. Craig R. Koester—Professor of New Testament, Luther Seminary. Dr. Koester is author of the Anchor Bible Commentary on Hebrews, *Revelation and the End of All Things*, and *Symbolism in the Fourth Gospel*. He is active in the Society for New Testament Studies, the Society of Biblical Literature, and the Catholic Biblical Association. An ordained minister of the Evangelical Lutheran Church in America, he is a former parish minister.

Segment 29: Dr. Joel B. Green—Dean of Academic Affairs and Professor of New Testament Interpretation, Asbury Theological Seminary. Dr. Green is author of *Salvation, Beginning with Jesus, Recovering the Scandal of the Cross*, and *The Gospel of Luke* in the New International Commentary of the New Testament. He is a United Methodist.

Segment 30: Art, words, and music.

Actors
Alain Browning
Connye Florance
Cecil Jones
Eun Joo Kho
Renee Lopez
Shelean Newman
Stella Reed
Rob Wilds

Roles of the Leader

JESUS IN THE GOSPELS looks closely at the Gospel texts and requires careful attention to detail. As a result, this approach to study requires the leader to pay careful attention to the roles played in helping the group make the most of the weekly session.

The Leader as Guide
The leader knows the aim of the study.

The aim of JESUS IN THE GOSPELS is stated in "Reading's Promise" on study manual page 5. "In the case of the Gospels attentive reading means bearing in mind that their purpose is to *form* their readers by the way they *inform* them about the subject matter. The Gospels achieve their purpose when we grasp enough of what they tell us about Jesus that we can be grasped by him."

The point of paying careful attention to detail in the Gospel texts is to see in the Gospels the Jesus who calls us to follow him. Imagine looking at a painting or another work of art. The more carefully you look, the more you change your angle of view, the more you are able to see what is there. Learning to see the Jesus who is there in the Gospels is the aim of this study.

To that end, a question in italics appears in the last section of each lesson in the study manual. The question in Lesson 1 asks, Who is the Jesus you bring to this study? The question in Lesson 30 asks, Who is the Jesus you take with you from this study? The questions in Lessons 2–29 ask in one way or another, Who is Jesus here in this Scripture? As the leader, you know the aim of these questions echoes the aim of the study.

The leader clears the way ahead for the group.

To help group members make the most of this study, the leader previews with them what to expect in each upcoming lesson. Do this each week at the close of the group session just before viewing Part II of the week's video segment.
- Highlight the things to look for in the daily assignment section of the study manual.
- Point out any notes, charts, or glossary items present in the lesson.
- Identify the locations of teal-colored Gospel Comparison symbols in the lesson. Call attention to the instructions at the top of each Gospel Comparison and be alert to when those instructions vary from instructions in the study manual.

- Encourage note-taking. Call attention to the words *note*, *notice*, and *observe* in the daily assignments. Refer to the steps under "Completing daily assignments" on study manual page 7 to guide group members in their daily study.

The leader keeps the focus on the Gospels.

In this study, the leader guides discussion. Most of the time this means posing the questions suggested in the leader guide. Sometimes this means being able to clarify the intent of a question. Sometimes this means navigating differences of opinions in order to stimulate rather than stifle fruitful thinking. Sometimes this means refocusing the conversation on the text before the group. Always this means resisting the temptation to lecture.

The Leader as Facilitator
The leader understands the components and the process of this study.

A group's ability to make use of the study manual and Gospel Comparisons as well as experience a meaningful weekly session reflects the leader's understanding and handling of the components and the session. The leader should be thoroughly familiar with the content of "A Word to the Reader" on study manual pages 6–7; "How to Use Gospel Comparisons" on Gospel Comparisons pages 4–7; and "The Weekly Group Process" on page 6 in this leader guide.

Individual daily study and weekly group study always move among three components: a study Bible, the study manual, and Gospel Comparisons. The leader's job is to facilitate this movement.

The leader prepares.

This is not material that can be prepared the night before. Likewise, the weekly group session cannot flow smoothly without prior planning.

First, prepare as a participant.
- Read and take notes on Scriptures daily, working through the suggestions of things to look for in each assignment. Set aside forty-five minutes to an hour on Days 1–5 and at least an hour on Day 6 for reading the commentary in the study manual. Expect all group members to prepare for the weekly session as you do.

Then prepare as the leader.

- Read the session plan in the leader guide. Since use of a hymn is suggested for the opening of each session, have hymnals available for singing or reading. If you determine the suggested hymn is unfamiliar to your group, choose an alternate.
- Preview Part I and Part II of the week's video segment. Locate the information about the video presenter in the leader guide. Make discussion questions available *after* the group has viewed the video. Be ready to clarify the questions if necessary.
- Determine time allotments for the various discussion activities and decide how you will form small groups. Often but not always the leader guide will make suggestions about when to form a certain number of groups or to talk in pairs or as a total group. Create new groups of people often and limit the time spent in total group discussion. This will ensure the widest possible interchange among the group and keep any one person from dominating the conversation—including the leader.
- Decide how to make available discussion questions and instructions to the group each week. Whether using paper, flipchart, whiteboard, or overhead, make arrangements to have everything ready and readable at the appropriate time in the group session.
- Note that the leader guide plans for each weekly session do not allot time for a break. Leaders will need to schedule a break whenever it seems to fit best in the flow of the discussion. Usually the most logical break point is following the discussion activities under the section "Beginning With Moses and All the Prophets."

The leader creates an environment for building community, accountability, and self-confidence on the part of each participant.

- Establish the practices of gathering in prayer, singing a hymn to start the session, closing with prayer and a video experience designed for reflection. These elements are complements to the disciplined study. Together this rhythm of worship and study can be the base around which community forms.
- Allow people to step hesitantly or even stumble along while others move with more ease. Encourage and affirm everyone just for taking the steps. Acknowledge effort and commitment.

The Leader as Director

Just as the director of a play is rarely seen on-stage during a performance, the leader of this study should lead from behind the scenes. Leading JESUS IN THE GOSPELS requires taking charge of things like setting up the room or ending a discussion. Sometimes these tasks call for being out front. But as much as possible during the weekly group sessions, the leader should work to stay out of the line of vision so others can see for themselves the Jesus in the Gospels. This means staying out of the way of the text and also staying out of the way throughout the study. **Remove your "I" so others' "eyes" can see.**

The work of directing this study carries with it some basic responsibilities:
Trusting
- Trusting the Gospels to reveal what matters about Jesus for our faith and witness.
- Trusting Jesus *in* the Gospels to come through people's study.
- Trusting the group to handle the challenges and the rewards of this study themselves.
- Trusting the content and the process of this study to open the Scriptures to fruitful learning.
- Trusting yourself: your effectiveness as the leader depends largely on how well you help others do their own work. Keep the emphasis on what you *do* with the group, not on what you *say* to the group.

Inviting
- Inviting group participants to think theologically not just inspirationally.
- Inviting participants to ask questions of the text—Why does each Gospel tell the story of Jesus differently?—but also to listen for the text's asking questions of them.
- Inviting participants to study carefully but at the same time to relax, to savor, to enjoy.

Affirming
- Affirming participants in the work they do, making clear that there is much to learn and think about. They may not (will not) "get" it all. And that's okay.
- Affirming that the study of Jesus in the Gospels may result in some uneasiness, some disquiet with the Jesus they encounter. Some uneasiness may prompt a more thoughtful, more deliberate discipleship.
- Affirming that not all questions raised by a study of Jesus in the Gospels will be answered. Some questions we'll have to live with.
- Affirming the expectation that when disagreement happens, you all agree to disagree agreeably.

An Information Meeting

Prepare

- Before scheduling an information meeting for those interested in learning about the JESUS IN THE GOSPELS study, read pages 6–7 in the study manual and pages 4–7 in Gospel Comparisons.

- Have the following items available for the meeting:
  - Copies of the JESUS IN THE GOSPELS handbook (available from the Cokesbury Seminars office in any quantity at no cost; call 800-672-1789 or 800-251-8591)
  - Copies of an interest form (see sample below)
  - Television set and VCR or DVD player
  - Video segment for Session 1
  - One complete set of JESUS IN THE GOSPELS materials available for persons to view

- Schedule the meeting (or meetings) on the church calendar. Coordinate childcare.

- Set up the room; check the equipment; cue the videotape (or prepare the DVD). Be early. Be ready.

Agenda

- Introduce the JESUS IN THE GOSPELS study and those who have been trained to lead it.

- Distribute the handbooks to everyone and review the following information:
  - the focus of the study (pages 4–8)
  - the importance of reading for detail (page 9)
  - the content and components of the study (pages 10–15)
  - the commitment to daily preparation (page 16)
  - the appropriate expectations to bring to the study (page 17)

- Show the video segment for Session 1 with Leander E. Keck, the writer of the study manual.

- Invite questions.

- Be sure to talk about the level of study required by JESUS IN THE GOSPELS as compared to DISCIPLE (page 3).

- Allow time at the close of the meeting for people to look through all the resources.

- Distribute interest forms. Close with prayer.

Interest Form	JESUS IN THE GOSPELS
	An in-depth study of the portraits of Jesus in the four Gospels. At the heart of the study is the question, Who is this Jesus?
	☐ YES! Please contact me with more information about JESUS IN THE GOSPELS.
	Name _____
	Address _____
	City/State/ZIP _____
	Telephone: Day (____) _____ Evening (____) _____

Group Orientation

Schedule group orientation one week prior to the first weekly session. Use the following schedule and procedure to guide the orientation process. Have the following items available:

- a handbook, a study manual, and a Gospel Comparisons for each person
- copies of "Read to Think Theologically," leader guide page 16
- a TV and VCR or DVD player
- a room with a table and enough chairs to accommodate the number of people attending

7:00 P.M.
Prayer

7:05 P.M.
Welcome the group.
- Introductions
- Affirm the group's commitment to study.
- Verify the meeting calendar.

7:15 P.M.
Introduce the study.
- Highlight main ideas in the handbook on pages 4–9.
- Show Video Segment 1 Part I.
- Explain that they will see the same video again in the first weekly group meeting.

7:30 P.M.
Distribute study manuals and Gospel Comparisons.
- Allow time for everyone to read "Reading's Promise" on study manual pages 4–5.
- Have everyone read "A Word to the Reader," study manual pages 6–7. Then explain the study manual format.
- Page through study manual Lesson 1 and see how each section works.
- Flip through several other lessons to sample the suggestions of things to look for. Emphasize the importance of note-taking and attention to detail (see also leader guide pages 5-6).
- Call attention to the note at the end of Lesson 1 on page 15. Mention that information not treated within a lesson may appear in brief notes or in charts.
- Call attention to the glossary on study manual pages 296–301. Locate the glossary words (identified by asterisks) in Lesson 1.

- Explain the need for a good study Bible. Explore study aids in the Bible that would be particularly useful for this study, especially footnotes, and annotations. Mention that daily assignments do occasionally include readings from the Apocrypha.
- Establish a plan of mutual prayer support.
- Recommend praying the prayer psalm aloud to close daily study.

7:45 P.M.
Introduce Gospel Comparisons.
- Call attention to the introductory article on pages 4–7 in Gospel Comparisons. Allow time for everyone to read the whole article.
- Respond to questions on how to use Gospel Comparisons.

7:55 P.M.
Practice taking notes on Lesson 1, Day 2.
- Call attention to the four steps listed on page 7 in the study manual under "Completing Daily Assignments."
- Have everyone read the Scripture assignment for Day 2 in Lesson 1, study manual page 8, following the four steps.

8:15 P.M.
Explain the weekly group schedule and process.
- Discuss related issues—meeting location, video setup, childcare arrangements, refreshment schedule.
- Distribute and scan "Read to Think Theologically."

8:20 P.M.
Review assignment for Lesson 1.
- Hear and record prayer concerns.

8:25 P.M.
Covenant together to
- Be present every week for weekly meetings but faithful to study when absent.
- Pray daily for one another.
- Prepare daily by reading and taking notes.
- Participate in every session by both listening and discussing.

8:30 P.M.
Dismiss.

Read to Think Theologically

1 Approach Bible reading as an active dialogue between yourself and each of the writers of the Bible.

2 Dialogue is possible only if the reader is willing to be questioned by the Bible; there is no dialogue at all without the possibility of being converted to biblical faith.

3 Being a participant in an ongoing dialogue with the Bible puts the reader in conversation with other readers as well as with the writer.

4 Bible reading is an occasion for basic decisions about life if the reader is willing to listen openly to what the writer says about God's involvement with his creatures and to make an honest response to what the writer says.

5 The Bible can speak for itself if it has a chance to do so.

6 Genuine listening requires paying close attention to the text.

7 The Bible's inner core of meaning opens up when the reader stops taking the text for granted and begins to ask why it says what it does.

8 The seriousness of our reading of the Bible can be measured by the extent to which we permit significant disagreement.

9 The Bible is usually more prepared to face tough problems than are its readers.

10 Finding Jesus in the Old Testament is not nearly so important as finding the Old Testament in Jesus.

Adapted from *Taking the Bible Seriously*, by Leander E. Keck, © Copyright by Abingdon Press.
Permission is granted to copy this page for JESUS IN THE GOSPELS use.

Session Guides 1—30

1 Jesus *in* the Gospels

Coming Together (30 minutes)

- Gather with prayer.
- Sing or read the words of a hymn.
  "Be Thou My Vision" or "At the Name of Jesus"
- Prepare to view video.
  Host: Priscilla Pope-Levison, Professor of Theology, Seattle Pacific University.
  Presenter: Leander E. Keck, Winkley Professor of Biblical Theology Emeritus, Yale University Divinity School, writer of the JESUS IN THE GOSPELS study manual.
  Listen for the aim of the Gospels and how they achieve their aim.
- View Video Segment 1 Part I.
- Discuss after viewing:
  How do the Gospels inform us about Jesus? What early Christian convictions about the meaning of Jesus were shared by the Gospel writers? What were some consequences of putting oral traditions into writing? How are we to read the Gospels?

Beginning With Moses and All the Prophets (45 minutes)

- The assumption that form follows function guides approach to study in JESUS IN THE GOSPELS. That is, how something is told reflects why it is told. With that idea in mind, work through the week's Scriptures one day at a time. Refer to notes and observations made during preparation.

  Day 1—Work in groups of three or four. For each passage, identify the form the writer used to record the events, talk about what the choice of form indicates about how the passage was intended to be used, and talk about your response to the form and the tone of each passage.

  Day 2—Invite one person from each group to shift to another group. Discuss these questions: What stood out for you in the Deuteronomy passages about what is to be remembered and why? What ways or forms did the writers of 2 Timothy and 1 Peter use to present what is to be remembered about Jesus and the purpose for remembering? Certain small words within this day's passages point to the reasoning within the passages. Scan each passage looking for use of the words *so that*, *for*, and *so as* connecting what is to be remembered and the purpose for the remembering. How did use of these words serve the writer's purpose?

  Day 3—Form new groups of three or four to consider how the writer of these sermons took account of setting and audience in determining what he emphasized about Jesus. For each passage, review Scripture and daily notes to answer these questions: What is the setting? What is said about Jesus? How does the writer fashion what he says to fit the listeners? To what in their experience does the writer appeal?

Day 4—Work in two groups. First, review the meaning of *tradition.* Then, answer this question about each passage: What aspect (or aspects) of Jesus did the writer of this passage consider important enough to be handed on as tradition? After considering each passage discuss this question: What purposes were these traditions to fulfill?

Day 5—In the same two groups discuss this question: What is your understanding of what constitutes the gospel? Then identify the gospel in the passages from Hebrews and 1 John. Where and how is the gospel expressed in these passages?

- Now in the total group respond to this question: What insights, wisdom, guidance might we glean from study of the connection between how a story is told and why it is told that can help us hand on to others the gospel we have received?

Jesus *in* the Gospels (45 minutes)

- Clarify assumptions about the Gospels that underlie this study. In groups of three review the note "The Gospels" on study manual page 15. Consult the glossary on study manual pages 296–301 for definitions of Q, M, and L. Then discuss this question: How can knowing the kind of writing the Gospels are help us know what to expect from them? Next, clarify certain terms that will recur throughout the study: *Canon, Gospels, Synoptics, Evangelists.* Hear one another define the terms and the relationship among them.

- Take a few minutes now for persons to describe what they are feeling and what they are wondering as they undertake a study of Jesus in the Gospels. Recall that the study manual makes the point that the Gospels and the Jesus in the Gospels intend to do more than give answers to the questions we already have; both Jesus and the Gospels intend to question us. Talk about what this point says to the assumptions and expectations persons bring to the study.

- Distinguish the *gospel* from *Gospels.* Recall that people believed the gospel before they had Gospels. What is the gospel they believed? In the total group recall how the study manual defines and explains the *gospel* and puts the gospel message into words. Then hear Paul's core gospel message read aloud from 1 Corinthians 15:3-8 on study manual page 12. Invite members of the group to reflect silently on this question: How has the core gospel message that Paul received and handed on been handed on to me? Then respond to the question in pairs.

Do You Want to Become His Disciples, Too? (20 minutes)

- Call attention to the question, "What will we hand on to our children, and to their children?" on study manual page 8. Why is it so crucial to hand on the Gospels' witness to Jesus that we have received? What particular challenges face us in accomplishing this task?

- In pairs hear each other's written response to the question on study manual page 14, *Who is the Jesus you bring with you to this study?*

Going Forth (10 minutes)

- Preview Lesson 2. Hear prayer concerns.
- Pray in unison the prayer on study manual page 15.
- View Video Segment 1 Part II.

2 When Words Became Events

Coming Together (30 minutes)

NOTES

- Gather with prayer.
- Sing or read the words of a hymn.
  "O Come, O Come, Emmanuel" or "Come, Thou Long-Expected Jesus"
- Prepare to view video.
  Presenter: Dale C. Allison, Jr., Errett M. Grable Professor of New Testament and Christian Origins, Pittsburgh Theological Seminary. Listen for ways Matthew alludes to or draws from the Old Testament.
- View Video Segment 2 Part I.
- Discuss after viewing:
  Why did Matthew include the genealogy? What is the significance of the names he included? Why does the outline of Matthew's first few chapters parallel the life of Moses in the Old Testament?

Beginning With Moses and All the Prophets (45 minutes)

- Explore the significance of the word *fulfill* in Matthew 1–2. Work in two groups to identify the Old Testament passages quoted in Matthew 1:23; 2:6; 2:15; 2:18; 2:23. Begin by looking up the five passages in the Old Testament books they come from. Read the headings of chapters surrounding the Old Testament passages, consult the annotations, and scan introductions to the books to get an idea of (1) why, (2) when, and (3) to whom the passages were written. What was the prophet's original purpose in speaking the words in each passage? What is Matthew's purpose in claiming that what was spoken by these prophets was fulfilled in Jesus? Finally, hear in the total group any words persons came up with to make the same point as the word *fulfill*.
- Study Matthew's use of the genealogy to place Jesus within Israel's history. Assign to each person in the group one of the following names in the genealogy: Abraham, Isaac, Jacob, Tamar, Rahab, Ruth, David, the wife of Uriah (Bathsheba), Solomon, Hezekiah, Josiah, Joseph, Mary. Allow time for persons to recall (or look up in their Bibles) something about the names they were assigned. Then read aloud Matthew 1:1-17, pausing after speaking each assigned name. During the pause after each name, a person tells briefly what is known about the biblical figure named. At the end of this process discuss these questions: What do the figures in Matthew's genealogy represent in terms of Israel's history? Why are they important? And why is it important for Matthew that Jesus be connected to them? Conclude by talking about why you think Matthew included women in Jesus' genealogy.
- Matthew introduces as the "son of David" both Jesus (1:1) and Joseph (1:20). Review the readings for Day 5 and daily notes to identify the substance and meaning of God's promises to David. Then discuss this

question: Why does Matthew make explicit the connection between Jesus the Messiah and God's promise to David in the Old Testament? Conclude by reading aloud Jeremiah 23:5-6.

When Words Became Events (45 minutes)

- From its beginning, Matthew's Gospel tells readers who Jesus is and points to his meaning. Working individually, scan Matthew 1–2, looking at the chapters as a whole to identify clues to the significance of Jesus. Hear in the total group what clues persons identified.
- The study manual suggests that to understand Matthew 1–2, we should put our own questions aside, at least to begin with. Rather, we should look for what the Gospel writer is telling us and for the kind of response expected of us. Discuss these questions: What questions do you have about the birth and infancy of Jesus that Matthew leaves unanswered? Why do you think Matthew does not answer those questions? What questions about Jesus does Matthew answer? What response do you think Matthew expects us to make to his account of Jesus' birth?
- In Chapters 1–2 Matthew identifies Jesus as Messiah and supports that claim by showing Jesus in relation to Israel, to Scripture, and to God. Review notes made on readings and on "Jesus' Identity Stated" on study manual pages 19–20 to talk about those three relationships. Work in three groups to locate passages from Matthew 1–2 that indicate Jesus' identity in relation to Israel (Group 1), Jesus' identity in relation to Scripture (Group 2), Jesus' identity in relation to God (Group 3). Have the groups come together after identifying the passages and respond to this question: In light of your work, why do you think Matthew states Jesus' identity as Messiah in terms of relationships?
- Recall these concluding remarks in "So Then" on study manual page 21: "Celebrating this birth is easy. Too easy, in fact, when we neglect the dark underside of this introduction to Jesus . . ." What does Matthew accomplish by including the darker elements in the story of Jesus' birth and infancy? What more about Jesus' identity do we know because we know about these threats to Jesus so early in his story?

Do You Want to Become His Disciples, Too? (20 minutes)

- In this section the study manual states that the divine promise often is kept in ways we do not expect. Hear what persons cited as examples from their own experience. What makes trusting God's promises difficult when they are kept in ways we do not expect?
- Think back over the week's study of Matthew 1–2. What claims would you say Matthew makes about Jesus in this birth story?
- In pairs hear responses to the question on study manual page 22, *What claim does the Jesus in Matthew's "birth story" make on you?*

Going Forth (10 minutes)

- Preview Lesson 3. Hear prayer concerns.
- Pray in unison the prayer on study manual page 22.
- View Video Segment 2 Part II.

3 Celebrating Beginnings

Coming Together (30 minutes)

- Gather with prayer.
- Sing or read the words of a hymn.
  "Go, Tell It on the Mountain" or "Angels We Have Heard on High"
- Prepare to view video.
  Presenter: Sarah J. Tanzer, Professor of New Testament and Early Judaism, McCormick Theological Seminary.
  Listen for clues in the major themes of Luke 1–2 to God's purpose in Jesus.
- View Video Segment 3 Part I.
- Discuss after viewing:
  Identify the major themes in Luke 1–2. What do Luke's major themes suggest about God's purpose in Jesus? What does the idea that Chapters 1–2 are an introduction to Luke *and* Acts say about Luke's purpose in telling the story of Jesus' birth?

Beginning With Moses and All the Prophets (45 minutes)

- Explore Luke's distinctive angle of vision on the birth and infancy of Jesus. First, scan Luke 1–2 to identify where the tone of the passage is joyful. What does Luke's emphasis on the celebration accompanying Jesus' birth say about who Jesus is in Luke's Gospel? What would the church miss in its observance of Advent and Christmas without Luke 1–2?
- Trace Luke's use of the word *favor, favored,* or *favorably* in Chapters 1–2, using the New Revised Standard Version. Consult other translations to compare how those ideas are expressed. Then see how the word *favor* is used in selected Old Testament passages (using the NRSV): Genesis 6:8; Exodus 34:9; Ruth 2:10; 1 Samuel 1:18. What does it mean for the angel to call Mary "favored"? What does it mean to say "God favors"? What do you think Luke is trying to say in using those words so frequently to tell the birth story of Jesus?
- Focus on Luke's distinctive use of the Old Testament in telling the stories of the births of John and Jesus.
  (1) Referring to notes made on Day 2 readings, talk about the similarities between the story of Samuel and Luke's account of the births of John and Jesus. Hear what similarities persons noted among the song of Hannah (1 Samuel 2:1-10), the Magnificat (Luke 1:46-55), and the Benedictus (Luke 1:68-79). What is Luke saying about Jesus by showing a connection between Hannah's prayer and the prayers of Mary and Zechariah? How is the theme of reversal expressed in the three prayers? And why is that theme part of Luke's story of Jesus' birth?
  (2) Scan the Day 3 readings from Isaiah and refer to daily notes to identify the word pictures the prophet used to convey God's promise of restoration.

How might these Scriptures have nurtured Simeon's and Anna's hopes for the salvation of Israel? How might the Scriptures have informed Luke's understanding of the meaning of the births of John and Jesus?

■ In groups of three compare the annunciation stories of John and Jesus in Luke 1–2. Using **GC 3-1** talk about similarities in the two stories. How does Luke make clear the roles of John and Jesus by telling about their births in similar ways? Compare 1:59 and 2:21. Why was it important for Luke to situate John and Jesus in devout Jewish life?

Celebrating Beginnings (45 minutes)

■ Compare aspects of Luke's account of Jesus' birth to Matthew's account, using **GC 3-G**. Begin by forming two groups: Group 1 to compare Matthew 1 and Luke 1; Group 2 to compare Matthew 2 and Luke 2. (1) First, have groups scan their assigned chapters in **GC 3-G**, highlighting and making notes with these questions in mind: Who are the people each Gospel writer includes in the story of Jesus' birth? Why are they important for understanding who Jesus is? Each Gospel writer emphasizes certain people associated with Jesus. How does that emphasis contribute to each Gospel's distinctive message about Jesus? What do you make of each Gospel's portrayal of Joseph and Mary? (2) After both groups have completed the previous discussion, have them once again scan their assigned chapters in **GC 3-G**, highlighting and making notes with these questions in mind: How do dreams in Matthew and the Holy Spirit in Luke function in the telling of Jesus' birth? What are similarities and differences in their functions? (3) Now hear in the total group what persons learned about each Gospel writer's distinctive telling of Jesus' birth. How does each Gospel convey what the writer considers is important about Jesus?

■ Talk about the importance of the Temple in Luke. What is Luke's purpose in giving the Temple a prominent place in the story of Jesus' birth? Then read Luke 2:22-24, 39-41. Now discuss this question: By emphasizing the Temple and the Jewish piety of Mary and Joseph in Chapters 1–2, what does Luke want his readers to understand about Jesus?

■ Call attention to the statement under "So Then" on study manual page 30 that Matthew and Luke do not narrate Jesus' birth at all. How are Matthew 1–2 and Luke 1–2 both more than and less than "birth stories"?

Do You Want to Become His Disciples, Too? (20 minutes)

■ In groups of three or four talk about why Matthew 1–2 and Luke 1–2 sometimes generate more argument over what really happened than praise of God for the coming of John and Jesus.

■ How would your understanding of Jesus' birth be affected if the church celebrated Christmas and Easter together?

■ In pairs hear responses to the question on study manual page 31, *What aspects of Luke's birth story combine to express your faith in Jesus?*

■ Conclude by standing and singing Stanza 1 of "Joy to the World."

Going Forth (10 minutes)

■ Preview Lesson 4. Hear prayer concerns.
■ Pray in unison the prayer on study manual page 31.
■ View Video Segment 3 Part II.

4 The Wilderness Voice

Coming Together (30 minutes)

NOTES

- Gather with prayer.
- Sing or read the words of a hymn.
  Stanzas 1 and 2 of "Come, Ye Sinners, Poor and Needy" or "O Jesus, I Have Promised"
- Prepare to view video.
  Presenter: Amy-Jill Levine, E. Rhodes and Leona B. Carpenter Professor of New Testament Studies, Vanderbilt University Divinity School.
  Listen for what is said about the relationship between John the Baptist's mission and Jesus' mission. Also listen for the connection between John and Elijah.
- View Video Segment 4 Part I.
- Discuss after viewing:
     What was central to the message of John the Baptist? What about John's message prompted the Gospels to connect him to the prophet Elijah in particular? How do the Gospels see John the Baptist as a messianic forerunner? If both John and Jesus insisted on repentance, what is the difference in their message and their mission?

Beginning With Moses and All the Prophets (60 minutes)

- Focus on the readings for Days 1–4 to get a clear picture of John the Baptist, his mission, and his message. Form four groups and work in the following ways:
  (1) Assign each of the four groups one of the four passages from Mark listed for Day 1. Using daily notes, discuss these questions about each passage: What does the passage tell you about John? What does the passage tell you about Jesus? What does the passage tell you about the mission of John and its significance for understanding the mission of Jesus?
  (2) Next assign each of the four groups one of the following passages: Malachi 4; 1 Kings 17:1–19:18; 2 Kings 1; Sirach 48:1-14. Using daily notes, discuss these questions about each passage: What does the passage tell you about Elijah? Based on this passage, what parallels do you see between Elijah and John the Baptist?
  (3) Have the four groups turn to GC 4-1 and refer to their daily notes. Allow persons a few minutes to discuss insights and questions that came during daily preparation as they compared the four Gospels' introductions and interpretations of John the Baptist. What is the significance of Mark's omission of the content of John's preaching? What is the significance of Luke's inclusion of John's words spelling out what repentance entails? Compare the Gospels' use of Isaiah 40—What do the variations in the length of the quotation say about each Gospel's understanding of how

John the Baptist fulfills Isaiah's promise? Why do you think John's Gospel has John the Baptist himself claim to fulfill the words of Isaiah? Identify the audience to whom John preaches in each Gospel. How does knowing who his audience is affect our understanding of John's preaching? (4) Bring together the four groups to summarize what the Gospels say about John the Baptist. Hear one person at a time describe in a word or phrase who John the Baptist is according to Mark. Then hear one person at a time describe in a word or phrase who John the Baptist is according to Matthew. Then hear words or phrases describing who John the Baptist is according to Luke, and finally according to John.

The Wilderness Voice (30 minutes)

- Shift focus from John the Baptist to Jesus, whose significance makes John important in the first place. Begin by inviting one person to read aloud Matthew 3:1-2 and another person to read Matthew 4:17. For Matthew, what is the significance of hearing Jesus preach with words identical to John's words? Now hear Acts 19:1-7 read aloud. While Matthew indicates no distinction between John's preaching and Jesus' preaching, Paul makes a clear distinction between John's baptism and baptism in Jesus' name. How do you account for that?
- Work in groups of three or four with **GC 4-2**. Hear the similarities and differences persons observed in the two passages. How does each Gospel convey Jesus' view of John's role in relationship to himself? Given how the Gospels describe John the Baptist, what do you think motivated John's question to Jesus in Matthew 11:2-3? Why was Jesus not what John expected? Why do both Gospels record Jesus' speaking highly of John and also contrasting his mission with John's mission?
- Both John and Jesus use the language of Isaiah to characterize their respective missions. Assign six people to read aloud the Isaiah passages associated with John and with Jesus from the week's assignments. Read in this sequence: Isaiah 40:3-5; 29:18-19; 40:6-8; 35:5-6; 40:9-11; 61:1. Then discuss this question: How do these passages from Isaiah both connect and differentiate the missions of John and Jesus?

Do You Want to Become His Disciples, Too? (20 minutes)

- How would you say John prepared the way for Jesus' mission?
- Call attention to the observation on study manual page 39 that at times John's question to Jesus may also be our question: "Are you the Coming One or shall we look for someone else?" Talk in pairs about a time when John's question was yours, too.
- Still in pairs hear responses to the questions on study manual page 39, *Who is this Jesus John the Baptist points to?* and *What is it about Jesus that makes John important?*

Going Forth (10 minutes)

- Preview Lesson 5. Hear prayer concerns.
- Pray in unison the prayer on study manual page 39.
- View Video Segment 4 Part II.

5 Gifted by the Spirit and Tested by the Choices

Coming Together (30 minutes)

- Gather with prayer.
- Sing or read the words of a hymn.
  "Lord, Who Throughout These Forty Days" or Stanzas 2 and 3 of "What a Friend We Have in Jesus"
- Prepare to view video.
  Presenter: Susan R. Garrett, professor of New Testament, Louisville Presbyterian Theological Seminary.
  Listen for how testing of the righteous was understood in Mark's time and for the role and purpose of God and of Satan in Jesus' temptations.
- View Video Segment 5 Part I.
- Discuss after viewing:
    How were trials of the righteous understood in Mark's time? Why was Jesus tempted right after he was baptized? What was God's role and purpose in Jesus' being tempted? What role did Satan play? What was the outcome of Jesus' having endured temptation? What can we draw from Jesus' example when facing temptation?

Beginning With Moses and All the Prophets (45 minutes)

- Focus on the baptism and temptation accounts in the Day 1 Scriptures.
  (1) In groups of three or four using **GC 5-1**, notes made on daily readings, and study manual pages 42–44, identify differences in the three Synoptic accounts. What do those differences say about what each writer wants to emphasize about Jesus? What did you observe about the link between the baptism and the temptation? What more is there to the link than closeness on the page? What emphasis is Luke making both in the way he records the genealogy and in his placement of it between his account of the baptism and the temptation?
  (2) Look next at John's account of the baptism in John 1:29-34. How does it compare in tone and intention with the Synoptics' accounts? Scan John 1:1-18 to get in mind the content and sequence of John's presentation of Jesus. Then talk briefly about the Jesus John presents. Why do you think John did not include a temptation story? What difference does that make in the way you picture Jesus?
- Luke gives special emphasis to the Spirit as is evident in his story of Jesus' preaching in his hometown synagogue. In groups of two review notes on Luke 4:16-30 and on 1 Kings 17:1; 18:1-2; 2 Kings 5:1-14. Trace the buildup of tension resulting from Jesus' comments after reading from Isaiah. What message was Jesus sending by each comment? What message did his hearers hear and why did they react so strongly? What angle on Jesus is Luke emphasizing in his references to the experiences of Elijah and Elisha? What is important in Luke 4:16-30 about the coming of the Spirit to Jesus?

- Temptation is talked about in different ways in the Day 5 readings. In groups of four using ▮GC 5-2▮, hear persons' responses to comparing Mark's and Luke's interpretations of the parable of the sower. How do the differences in detail affect the telling and the impact of the story? How does the parable address temptation? Where is temptation present in the passage about Jesus in the garden? To what temptation does Peter succumb in Luke 22:31-34?

Gifted by the Spirit and Tested by the Choices (45 minutes)

- Study the three temptations reported by Matthew and Luke. In groups of four, using ▮GC 5-3▮ and ideas from "The Triple Temptations" on study manual pages 44–45, identify the three temptations one at a time in each Gospel. Say what the issue is in each temptation. Then consider Jesus' responses to the temptations. Referring to notes on Day 2 readings, describe the source and situation from which Jesus drew Scripture for his response to each temptation. What is the connection in the temptation experience between Jesus and Israel? Looking again at ▮GC 5-3▮, hear persons' observations about the difference in sequence of the second and third temptations. What difference, if any, do you think the sequence makes in how each writer wants to present Jesus? What does the sequence say about the lure of temptation? How does the difference in climax in the accounts affect your understanding of Jesus?
- Read silently the paragraph under "They Have No Wine" on study manual page 40. The Old Testament passages from Days 3 and 4 illustrate the points made in that paragraph. Work in two groups on the passages one at a time: Identify the persons and situation in the passage, the choices being presented, the choices made, and the reasons for the choices made. Then say how the persons and the actions in the passage illustrate particular points made under "They Have No Wine."
- Now hear guidance the New Testament offers us in our vulnerability to temptation. Read aloud Hebrews 2:18 on study manual page 40. Form three groups: Group 1—Hebrews 2:14-18; 4:14-16; 12:3-17; Group 2—1 Corinthians 10:1-13; Group 3—James 1. Invite each group to review the assigned passage(s) identifying statements of guidance, support, and assurance that can help persons facing temptation. In the total group hear what each group discovered. What temptations do we resist if we heed the exhortations in Hebrews 12:12-17?

Do You Want to Become His Disciples, Too? (20 minutes)

- The issues Jesus faced appear also in our temptations though in different forms. Recall the three issues in Jesus' temptations. Then discuss this question: In what forms, shapes, guises, words do those same issues confront us? Jesus settled the issues before he began his ministry. In what sense can disciples also make choices that settle issues?
- What do the stories of Jesus' baptism and temptation tell us that is important for the ways we understand Jesus?
- In pairs hear each other's written response to the question on study manual page 47, *In what ways does the tempted/tested Jesus challenge and comfort you?*

Going Forth (10 minutes)

- Preview Lesson 6. Hear prayer concerns.
- Pray in unison the prayer on study manual page 47.
- View Video Segment 5 Part II.

6 When God's Reign Becomes Real

Coming Together (30 minutes)

- Gather with prayer.
- Sing or read the words of a hymn.
  "Jesus Shall Reign" or "Rejoice, the Lord Is King"
- Prepare to view video.
  Presenter: Paul N. Anderson, Professor of Biblical and Quaker Studies, George Fox University.
  Listen for what Jesus meant by the phrase "the kingdom of God" and what his contemporaries thought about his talk of the Kingdom.
- View Video Segment 6 Part I.
- Discuss after viewing:
  What expectations of the kingdom of God did Jesus challenge? According to Jesus, how does the way of the Kingdom manifest itself? What kind of response does the Kingdom require? Identify each Gospel writer's particular insight into what the kingdom of God is like. How do these insights help us understand what the kingdom of God means?

Beginning With Moses and All the Prophets (45 minutes)

- Key questions in this week's study are these: What is it about the kingdom of God that prompts Jesus to speak of it with parables? and What about parables makes them appropriate for talking about the kingdom of God? With these questions in mind, consider the different ways God's kingdom or kingship is imaged in Scriptures other than the Gospels.
  (1) Assign these readings from Days 1, 2, and 3 to three groups: Group 1—Psalms 93; 95; 97; Group 2—Zechariah 14:9-11; Judges 8:22-23; 1 Samuel 8; Tobit 13; Group 3—1 Corinthians 15:35-57; Galatians 5:16-26; Revelation 11:15-20. Review notes and observations made during preparation to discuss these questions: What characteristics of God's kingdom or God's kingship do the images in these passages convey? How are people expected to respond to God's kingdom or kingship?
  (2) Turn now to the Gospels. Invite someone to read aloud Mark 1:14-15; Matthew 4:12-17; and Luke 17:20-21. Keeping in mind the various Scriptures about God's kingdom and kingship, talk in the total group about clues to why the "kingdom of God" is central to Jesus' message.
- Form two groups to look at how the Gospel readings and Old Testament readings for Day 5 accent the demands of the Kingdom.
  (1) Consider the passages from Exodus and Leviticus alongside the Gospel accounts of Jesus and the rich young man. Summarize the demands of the Law according to the passages from Exodus and Leviticus. How does the rich young man understand the demands of the Law? How does Jesus understand them? How does Jesus understand the relationship between the demands of the Law and the demands of God's kingdom? What aspects of God's kingdom make riches an obstacle for those seeking the Kingdom?

(2) Compare the Gospel passages for Day 5 looking for more clues to the demands of God's kingdom. The Synoptics place Jesus' welcoming of the children and proclamation that the Kingdom belongs to "such as these" just before the story of the rich young man. In what way do the stories of Jesus and the children and Jesus and the rich man—read *together*—inform your understanding of the demands of God's kingdom?
(3) In light of what you have learned thus far about the idea of God's kingdom or kingship, complete this sentence: The kingdom of God is . . .

When God's Reign Becomes Real (45 minutes)

- Begin working with Jesus' kingdom parables by reviewing the Gospel readings for Day 4, daily notes, and "God's Kingship and Jesus' Parables" on study manual pages 52–53. Use these questions in groups of three or four to guide discussion: How is the word picture in a parable essential to the meaning of the parable? What makes these parables appropriate for speaking of God's kingdom? Why do ordinary images succeed in communicating the extraordinary nature of God's kingdom?
- Invite persons to choose one of Jesus' kingdom parables from this week's readings, read it, and think of an alternate word picture that conveys the sense of Jesus' parable. Allow time for persons to write their own parables using their alternate word pictures. In the total group hear what persons have written.
- Form new groups of three or four to work with the parable of the sower. Have the group scan the last paragraph of the glossary entry *Allegorical Interpretation* on study manual page 296. Using **GC 6-1** and daily notes, discuss similarities and differences in the Synoptics' interpretations of the parable. How does Luke's omission of the various yield amounts affect the meaning of the parable? How does Mark's inclusion of Jesus' rebuke of the disciples at the beginning of the passage affect the interpretation of the parable? Hear other insights.
- Turn to **GC 6-G** to address the question, Why parables? Review what the study manual says about the Greek word *hina* on page 53. Still in groups of three or four identify similarities and differences in the three passages in **GC 6-G**. How does each Gospel writer understand the purpose of Jesus' speaking in parables? Jesus' parables challenge the imagination because God's kingdom challenges the way we picture the world and our relation to God. In the total group talk about how the idea of God's kingdom or kingship challenges the way we picture the world and the way we relate to God.

Do You Want to Become His Disciples, Too? (20 minutes)

- Reread the paragraph under "Do You Want to Become His Disciples, Too?" on study manual page 55 and note the statement "Being a disciple takes imagination." In light of Jesus' use of parables and keeping in mind the lesson title, how do you understand that statement?
- Read aloud in unison the Lord's Prayer from Matthew 6:9-13. What does it mean to order our life so that it accords with God's will even before God's reign is acknowledged everywhere?
- Hear responses to the question on study manual page 55, *What insights into Jesus do you get through the parables he told about God's reign?*

Going Forth (10 minutes)

- Preview Lesson 7. Hear prayer concerns.
- Pray in unison the prayer on study manual page 55.
- View Video Segment 6 Part II.

7 Called and Commissioned

Coming Together (30 minutes)

- Gather with prayer.
- Sing or read the words of a hymn.
  "Jesus Calls Us" or "Here I Am, Lord"
- Prepare to view video.
  Presenter: Bruce Chilton, Bernard Iddings Bell Professor of Religion, Bard College.
  Listen for descriptions of Jesus in the role of rabbi and for explanation of the purposes served by three groups related to Jesus—followers, disciples, apostles.
- View Video Segment 7 Part I.
- Discuss after viewing:
  How did Jesus carry out his role as rabbi to his followers? How would you describe the relationship between a rabbi and a disciple? How did each of these three groups serve Jesus' purpose: followers? disciples? apostles? What special purposes did the Twelve serve?

Beginning With Moses and All the Prophets (60 minutes)

- Consider what each of the four Gospels wants to tell the reader in its stories of how Jesus acquired his disciples. In groups of four follow these procedures for using GC 7-1 and notes from daily study: (1) Compare Mark 1:16-20 and Matthew 4:18-22 noting any differences in wording or information and noting what is emphasized about becoming a disciple. Repeat the process for comparing Mark 2:13-17; Matthew 9:9-13; Luke 5:27-28. (2) Then look at Luke 5:1-11. What does Luke want to tell us through this account? (3) Now hear one person read John 1:35-51 aloud while others follow in their Bibles. Describe the setting. Who is involved and what part does each person play in the story? What are the meanings under the words? What does John want to tell us about Jesus by the way he reports Jesus' acquiring disciples?
- Focus on Mark's portrayal of the disciples and their relationship to Jesus. Form three groups and assign selected Scriptures from Day 2. Instruct the groups to review the Scriptures and their notes from daily study and discuss the related questions: Group 1—Mark 3:13-19; 4:35-41; 6:7-13, 30-52; 8:1-21. What did Jesus appoint the twelve apostles to do? How would you describe the disciples' privilege in accompanying Jesus? Why do you think the disciples so often missed the point of what Jesus said and did? Group 2—Mark 8:34–9:1; 9:30-37; 10:32-45. What made Jesus' message hard for the disciples to hear and understand? Group 3—Mark 14:17-54, 66-72; 16:1-8. What evidence do you see that as well as not understanding Jesus, the disciples did not understand themselves? Now in the total group discuss this question:

What does the combination of the disciples' privilege and failure suggest about Mark's understanding of discipleship itself?

- To study Matthew's picture of the disciples and their relationship to Jesus, work in two groups on selected Matthew passages from Day 3 and discuss related questions: Group 1—Matthew 8:18-22; 9:35–11:1; Group 2—Matthew 13:16-17, 51-52; 15:29-39; 16:5-12; 17:14-21; 20:17-28; 28:16-20. How would you describe Jesus' attitude toward the disciples? the disciples' attitude toward Jesus? Now, using **GC 7-2** and **GC 7-3** answer this question: How does Matthew soften Mark's portrayal of the disciples?
- In two groups concentrate on Luke's portrayal of the disciples and their relationship to Jesus: Group 1—Luke 8:1-3; 9:1-50; Group 2—Luke 9:51–10:24; 17:1-10; 22:24-38. Use this question to guide study of the assigned passages: What were the disciples learning about Jesus, his mission, discipleship, and themselves in these stories from Luke?
- For John's portrayal of the disciples, concentrate not on the events themselves but on what John's report of the events reveals about the disciples' relationship to Jesus. Form three groups and assign Scripture: Group 1—John 6:1-21; 11:1-16; Group 2—John 6:41-71; 12:1-8; Group 3—John 13. Ask of each passage, What does this story tell us about the disciples' relationship to Jesus? Then in each group hear observations on suggestions (1), (2), and (3) under Day 5.

Called and Commissioned (30 minutes)

- The lesson emphasizes that discipleship is a deliberate positive response to Jesus' call. In pairs or threes examine Gospel passages that stress the seriousness of both the call and the response: Matthew 10:5-15, 32-42; 25:14-30; Mark 8:34–9:1 and Luke 9:57-62; Luke 14:25-35. Look for how the passages make these points: The invitation is not to be taken lightly, following Jesus is costly, following Jesus is a personal (individual) response to Jesus. Discuss this question: How do you understand the word *deliberate* in saying that discipleship is a deliberate positive response to Jesus' call?
- In the total group review "Discipleship and Mission" on study manual pages 60–62 and discuss this question: How does Jesus' mission define our mission as disciples today?

Do You Want to Become His Disciples, Too? (20 minutes)

- In the total group talk about the difference between being a fan of Jesus and being a follower of Jesus. First list the characteristics of a fan (in general) and a "fan" of Jesus. Next, on the basis of what you learned about the disciples Jesus called and taught, list the characteristics of a follower of Jesus. Now describe the necessary pliability of a follower of Jesus who is to be formed and re-formed by him.
- In pairs or threes hear persons' written responses to the question on study manual page 63, *What sense do you get of Jesus and his mission by the disciples he called and the way he called them?*

Going Forth (10 minutes)

- Preview Lesson 8. Hear prayer concerns.
- Pray in unison the prayer on study manual page 63.
- View Video Segment 7 Part II.

8 Mission With Healing Power

Coming Together (30 minutes)

- Gather with prayer.
- Sing or read the words of a hymn.
  "When Jesus the Healer Passed Through Galilee" or "Silence, Frenzied, Unclean Spirit"
- Prepare to view video.
  Presenter: Mark Allan Powell, Professor of New Testament, Trinity Lutheran Seminary.
  Listen for the connections between Jesus' healing ministry and his message about the kingdom of God and for how the Gospel writers spoke about and understood demon possession.
- View Video Segment 8 Part I.
- Discuss after viewing:
  How do the stories of healings and exorcisms illustrate Jesus' message that the kingdom of God has come near? What are the Gospel writers saying when they attribute sickness to demons? In what sense is the Christian's experience of the Kingdom both present and future?

Beginning With Moses and All the Prophets (45 minutes)

- To see how each Gospel presents Jesus' healing work from its own perspective, form four groups to examine selected passages from Days 1, 3, 4, 5: Group 1—Mark 1:40-45; 2:1-12; 3:1-6; 5:1-20; Group 2—Mark 5:21-34; 7:31-37; 8:22-26; 10:46-52; Matthew 8:1-4; Group 3—Matthew 8:5-13, 28-34; 9:1-8, 18-26, 27-31; Group 4—Matthew 9:32-34; Luke 17:11-19; John 4:46-53; 5:1-18. Instruct the groups to watch for what each Gospel writer emphasizes about Jesus' healing work and to use the following questions to guide their study: How did Jesus heal the person(s) or how did the healing happen? How did others on the scene respond? What happened as a result of the healing? On what occasions and why did Jesus take the initiative? What clues to Jesus' intentions come through in what he said? What words and actions were common to the various stories? What do you think each Gospel writer wanted to emphasize about Jesus in the way each told the healing stories?
- Examine Day 2 passages from the Old Testament and the Apocrypha to see what light they throw on the healing stories in the Gospels. In groups of three or four remind one another of the content of each of the passages and discuss these questions: How might these Scriptures have informed or inspired Jesus' healing actions? What understandings and assumptions in these Scriptures are reflected in the healing stories in the Gospels? Where do you see similarities in methods of healing and requirements of the person being healed in these passages and in the Gospel stories?

- To get some sense of the difference between exorcisms and healings, focus on four accounts of exorcism. In groups of four begin by using **GC 8-G** to study Mark 1:21-28 and Luke 4:31-37. Get the sense of the two accounts and identify differences. Then review Mark 5:1-20 and 9:14-29 with these questions in mind: What information and actions are common to all of the accounts? How do the demons or unclean spirits affect the persons in whom they reside? What is the significance of the demons' addressing Jesus? How does Jesus demonstrate his authority in each situation? How would you characterize the difference between exorcisms and healings?

Mission With Healing Power (45 minutes)

- In the total group look at passages in Acts that show the apostles and early followers of Jesus carrying on Jesus' healing work—Acts 3:1-10; 5:12-16; 8:5-8; 16:16-18; 19:11-12. In reading these accounts, watch and listen for echoes of the healing stories in the Gospels in terms of the need for healing, the authority by which the healing was done, people's expectation of the apostles, reports about the healings, the reactions of the healed, and the reactions of others. From these reports how would you say Jesus' mission was defining the mission of the disciples? Now cite some examples of how Jesus' followers through the centuries until today have extended his mission through healing, and say how the examples are expressions of the kind of person Jesus was.

- Using **GC 8-I**, compare three accounts of the same healing story to see what the writers want to say about the significance of Jesus. In groups of three hear what differences persons observed in the way the story is told and in the information included in or excluded from the story. How does the viewpoint of each writer come through in his choice of what information to include and what information to exclude from the story? What does each writer consider significant about Jesus and how does each account convey that significance?

- To grasp the idea that there is meaning in the way Gospel writers put material together, look at the placement of three healing stories in Mark. Form three groups and instruct the groups to concentrate on sections and passages numbered (1), (2), (3) on study manual page 67 one at a time, repeating these steps for each passage: Locate the passage in the Bible and check the surrounding verses to get an idea of the context. Scan the related material in the study manual. Answer this question: What point is Mark making by his placement of the passage?

Do You Want to Become His Disciples, Too? (20 minutes)

- Invite someone to read "They Have No Wine." In pairs discuss these questions: How does our physical self affect our inner and spiritual self? How does our inner self affect our body? What does caring for the body include? What does caring for the inner/spiritual self include?

- In pairs or groups of three or four respond in turn to the question on study manual page 70, *What do Jesus' healing activities say about who Jesus is?*

Going Forth (10 minutes)

- Preview Lesson 9. Hear prayer concerns.
- Pray in unison the prayer on study manual page 71.
- View Video Segment 8 Part II.

9 Conflicts Over Obedience

Coming Together (30 minutes)

- Gather with prayer.
- Sing or read the words of a hymn.
  "I Want a Principle Within" or "For the Healing of the Nations"
- Prepare to view video.
  Presenter: Pamela M. Eisenbaum, Associate Professor of Biblical Studies and Christian Origins, Iliff School of Theology.
  Listen for the three issues central to the debates between Jesus and the Pharisees and for the similarities between Jesus and the Pharisees.
- View Video Segment 9 Part I.
- Discuss after viewing:
  What three issues concerned both Jesus and the Pharisees in their debates? What did Jesus and the Pharisees have in common that made them more alike than different? What is Oral Torah and what are its functions?

Beginning With Moses and All the Prophets (45 minutes)

- Clarify the historical context of the Gospels before considering Gospel stories of Jesus' conflicts with those who understood obedience to God differently. Invite the group to read aloud the quotation in large type on study manual page 74 and to work in pairs to find an explanation for the statement by reviewing the three points on that page. Discuss this question: What are some cautions for Christians who read the Gospels and their accounts of Jesus' conflicts with the Pharisees?
- Look at four conflict stories from the perspective of the Pharisees and the perspective of Jesus. Form three groups and make these assignments: Group 1—Mark 2:1-22; 3:1-6; Group 2—Mark 2:1-12; Matthew 9:10-17; 12:9-14; Group 3—Luke 5:17-39; 6:6-11. Ask the groups to consider the stories one at a time, referring to study notes for Day 1 and "Mark 2:1–3:6" on study manual pages 74–76 and using these questions: What understandings about obedience and God's will underlie the issue at conflict— for the Pharisees? for Jesus? Then in the total group say where any or all of the concerns for *religious practice, interpretation of Scripture*, and *question of authority* are present in the conflict stories just studied.
- The Gospels report several conflicts over Sabbath. In groups of three use **GC 9-2** to study one of those stories. See related material on study manual pages 75–76. Hear what persons observed in their daily study about differences among the Gospel accounts in the disciples' actions, in the question of the Pharisees, and in Jesus' response to the question. What is the significance in Jesus' using examples from Scripture to justify the actions of the disciples? What is the message in Jesus' reference to the Son of Man as lord of the sabbath?

- To gain some insight into how Jesus' approach to Scripture differed from that of his critics who used the same Bible, form two groups to review these Scriptures: Exodus 20:1-17; Leviticus 24:1-9; Numbers 28:1-10; Deuteronomy 5:12-15; 1 Samuel 21:1-6; Hosea 5:13–6:6. On what points might Jesus and the scribes and Pharisees have differed in their understanding of what the Scriptures required in terms of obedience to God's will? What have you discovered about Jesus' distinct understanding of God's will in Scripture?

Conflicts Over Obedience (45 minutes)

- Each of the Synoptic Gospels reports conflict over the source of Jesus' healing power. In groups of three or four, working with Scriptures for Day 2, trace the connections among (1) the charge by the scribes and Pharisees that Jesus cast out demons by the power of Satan, (2) Jesus' responses to the charge, (3) the role of the Holy Spirit, (4) the defining of the unforgivable sin, and (5) accountability for words uttered. See also the last paragraph on study manual page 68 (Lesson 8). What constitutes blaspheming the Holy Spirit?
- Study Jesus' response to the question of the scribes and Pharisees about why his disciples eat without washing their hands. In groups of three or four focus on **GC 9-1**. Refer to study notes on Scriptures for Days 3 and 4 and related information under "Mark 7:1-23" on study manual pages 76–78. Hear what persons observed and highlighted as they compared the readings from Mark and Matthew during daily study. Identify what Jesus said to the Pharisees, to the crowd, and to the disciples. What point is Jesus making through the verses he quotes from Isaiah? According to Jesus, what does and does not defile? What constitutes obedience to God—for Jesus? for the scribes and Pharisees? Next reflect on the quotation in large type on study manual page 77 and discuss this question: What is the potential impact of the statement on how we view our own actions?
- Now in the total group talk about what guidance Romans 14 offers on how to be sensitive to other people's understanding of obedience.
- Explore the idea that Jesus' coming and his message bring division and conflict. In groups of three or four compare the readings in **GC 9-6** and decide what the message is. Next ask how the images of new cloth/old cloak and new wine/old wineskins address Mark 12:38-40 and Matthew 23. Then scan Luke 12:49-56 and respond to this question: How have you experienced or observed the truth of this Scripture?

Do You Want to Become His Disciples, Too? (20 minutes)

- Identify issues that underlie negative attitudes toward those who are determined to do right. What are the risks in being loyal to Jesus?
- In groups of four hear one another's written response to the question on study manual page 79, *What side of Jesus comes through in the reports of his conflicts with religious leaders?*

Going Forth (10 minutes)

- Preview Lesson 10. Hear prayer concerns.
- Pray in unison the prayer on study manual page 79.
- View Video Segment 9 Part II.

10 The Inaugural Word

Coming Together (30 minutes)

- Gather with prayer.
- Sing or read the words of a hymn.
  Stanza 3 of "We Would See Jesus" or "I Want to Walk as a Child of the Light"
- Prepare to view video.
  Presenter: Deborah Krause, Associate Professor of New Testament, Eden Theological Seminary.
  Listen for ways the Sermon on the Mount can be viewed as a summary of Jesus' message about the kingdom of God and Christian discipleship and for how the Beatitudes challenge the common understanding of *blessing*.
- View Video Segment 10 Part I.
- Discuss after viewing:
  What does Jesus' sermon teach about the kingdom of heaven? What does Jesus' sermon teach about Christian discipleship? How do the Beatitudes challenge the usual understanding of *blessing*? How would you describe the alternative worldview required of Jesus' followers?

Beginning With Moses and All the Prophets (45 minutes)

- To have the whole Sermon on the Mount in mind while concentrating on Matthew 5, hear the entire sermon read aloud. Prior to the meeting, invite readers (as few as three or as many as seven) and assign Scripture portions: Matthew 5:1-16, 17-32, 33-48; 6:1-18, 19-34; 7:1-14, 15-29. Readers will stand where they are and read without interruption or explanation one after the other. Explain to the group what is to happen and why. Ask the group simply to listen, not to follow in their Bibles and not to take notes. After the reading, as a group describe what life looks like when it turns Godward in response to the Kingdom.
- Compare sayings of Jesus in the Sermon on the Mount and the Sermon on the Plain. Use the chart on study manual page 80 to guide comparison of the printed passages in **GC 10-G**. Look for differences in wording, for content and emphases that appear in one Gospel and not in the other.
- Consider how Jesus' teachings reflect his Scripture. In groups of four or six focus on these Scriptures from Days 2 and 4: Psalms 24:1-6; 37; Micah 6:6-8; Leviticus 19:1-18; 24:10-23; Deuteronomy 5:1-21; 24:1-4; Isaiah 66:1-2. Listen or look for emphases in these Scriptures that are echoed in Jesus' teachings. Discuss this question: What conclusions do you draw about Jesus' teaching and the Scriptures he knew?
- To experience the high regard for God's law in Jesus' Scripture, form two groups to put Psalm 119:25-40 into their own words. Instruct Group 1 to study Psalm 119:25-32 and paraphrase it as a statement of loyalty to God's word and Group 2 to study 119:33-40 and paraphrase it as a

prayer for understanding God's commands. Then hear the groups read what they have written.

- In groups of four hear what persons discovered in daily study about how emphases in Scriptures for Day 5 are consistent with or similar to the Sermon on the Mount and the Sermon on the Plain.

The Inaugural Word (45 minutes)

- In the total group recall the main points in the note "The Beatitudes" on study manual page 89. Then in groups of three or four, using **GC 10-1** and notes from daily study, compare the "blessed" sayings in Matthew 5:3-12 with Luke 6:20-23. Instruct the groups to refer to the four points under "The Beatitudes" on study manual pages 83–84 in discussing the important differences between the two versions. Look then at Luke's woes in 6:24-26 (use the Bible or **GC 10-G**). Talk first about this question: What is Luke telling his readers by placing the woes after the blessings? Recall Moses' offer of a choice in Deuteronomy 11:26-28. How does the experience of choice differ from the experience of reversal? How does Jesus' promise of reversal of present circumstances address you and your group?
- Explore the relationship of *righteousness* (Matthew 5:20) and *perfection* (5:48). In groups of three or four, drawing on ideas from "On Doing the Will of God" on study manual page 84, answer these questions: What is the meaning of *perfect*? What is the meaning of *righteousness*? Then on the basis of the definition of *perfect*, describe the life that surpasses the righteousness of the scribes and Pharisees.
- Invite the group to review Matthew 5:17-20 and to say how these verses prepare for the teachings in 5:21-47. Why would these words of Jesus have been particularly important to his Jewish followers? What is Jesus saying here that Christian readers need to hear? Now form three groups to look at Matthew 5:21-47 with the understanding that Jesus' teaching does not set aside the Law but calls for a higher level of commitment. Begin by reading the quotation in large type on study manual page 85 and then consider six passages, one at a time: 5:21-26, 27-30, 31-32, 33-37, 38-42, 43-47. Ask this question of each situation: What constitutes the higher level of commitment called for by Jesus' teaching? Refer to "On Doing the Will of God" on study manual pages 85–87. Then discuss these questions: Why is obeying Jesus no easier than obeying Moses? What is Jesus doing in putting his teaching next to the Law in this way?

Do You Want to Become His Disciples, Too? (20 minutes)

- Talk together about how society defines the "good life." How do you define the "good life"? How does the Bible define the "good life"? How did Jesus define the "good life"? What are the marks of the "good life"?
- In pairs hear each other's response to the question on study manual page 88, *What picture of Jesus emerges in the Sermon on the Mount and the Sermon on the Plain?*

Going Forth (10 minutes)

- Preview Lesson 11. Hear prayer concerns.
- Pray in unison the prayer on study manual page 88.
- View Video Segment 10 Part II.

11 Counting on God

Coming Together (30 minutes)

- Gather with prayer.
- Sing or read the words of a hymn.
  "God Will Take Care of You" or "Great Is Thy Faithfulness"
- Prepare to view video.
  Presenter: Michael J. Brown, Assistant Professor of New Testament, Candler School of Theology.
  Listen for connections between Jesus' teachings on wealth and prayer and his Jewish Scriptures and traditions and for descriptions of the communal nature of the Lord's Prayer.
- View Video Segment 11 Part I.
- Discuss after viewing:
  What connections do you see between Jesus' criticism of accumulating wealth and Old Testament teachings on caring for the poor and loyalty to God? What attitudes and actions related to money serve wealth rather than God? What words and images in the Lord's Prayer reveal its roots in Jewish Scripture? What makes the Lord's Prayer the prayer of the community and of the individual?

Beginning With Moses and All the Prophets (45 minutes)

- Explore the relationship between ways of practicing religion and confidence in God. In pairs identify the religious practices in Matthew 6:1-18 and Jesus' teaching related to the practices. Then identify other acts of righteousness that Christians do to which Jesus' teachings here would also apply. Now in the total group discuss these questions: How does your believing that the God who sees in secret will reward you express confidence in God? What does the desire to be seen by God or to be seen by others have to do with the heart?
- Examine Old Testament roots of Jesus' teaching in Matthew 6. Form groups of four and assign these Scriptures from Day 2: Deuteronomy 15:7-11; 24:19-22; Proverbs 14:20-21, 31; Isaiah 58:1-12. Use these questions to guide review and discussion of each of the passages: What themes and teachings in this passage likely informed or influenced Jesus' teaching in Matthew 6? What does the passage teach about counting on God? Now invite persons to consider what Psalm 139:1-18 says to them as individuals about counting on God. Assign one third of the group Verses 1-6; another third, Verses 7-12; and the other third, Verses 13-18, with the instruction to read and reflect on the assigned verses and to be prepared individually to say how they can count on God and why.
- To consider how Jesus' teachings compare with other parts of the Bible, form two groups to study Day 5 Scriptures: Group 1—Job 31:24-28; Colossians 3:1-17; 1 Thessalonians 5:12-22; Group 2—Proverbs 13:25;

Sirach 29:8-23; 2 Corinthians 12:1-10; Philippians 4:10-13. Instruct the groups to identify differences and similarities in these teachings and Jesus' teachings.

Counting on God (45 minutes)

- Use **GC 11-1** to look at Matthew's and Luke's versions of the Lord's Prayer. In groups of three or four note the setting for each prayer and similarities and differences in the prayers. Recall explanations of each of the petitions in "Pondering the Model Prayer" on study manual pages 93–94. Then concentrate on three emphases: (1) Hallowing God's name—What does it mean to say that God is not to be confused with the world? (2) Petition for bread—List without discussion what we receive day by day from God. What does the list suggest about reliance on God? (3) Petition for forgiveness—What is the connection between our having offended God and our understanding of forgiveness?
- Make the point that prayer is something other than giving God a list of our needs. Invite participants to write a prayer in the form of a conversation with the parent in heaven, expressing both trust and needs. Before writing individual prayers, look together at 1 Kings 3:5-9 and 8:22-53 to see what characterizes these prayer-conversations of Solomon with God. Allow time for persons to write brief prayers. Then invite volunteers to read their prayers. Talk in the total group about how prayer-conversation requires a different way of thinking about prayer.
- Respond to Jesus' call to rethink and reorder the place of money and "things" in our lives. In groups of four use **GC 11-2** to compare Matthew 6:19-34 and Luke 12:13-34. Using notes from daily study and ideas from study manual pages 94–96, talk about what each passage says about the seductive dangers of wealth, about depending on God, and about the contrast between heaven and earth. Then discuss these questions: Why do the teachings of Matthew 6 make us uncomfortable? How can we begin to assess the difference between necessities and wants? If we put the Kingdom first, what happens in how we think about "these things"?
- With Luke 12:13-21 in mind, continue discussing the hold money has on us by looking at Scriptures for Day 4 from the Old Testament and the Apocrypha. Consider the passages one at a time. How does each passage address or express the seductive power of money—whether we have little or much? What is involved in making the choice between serving God and serving money?

Do You Want to Become His Disciples, Too? (20 minutes)

- Identify common concerns and needs that underlie the anxieties of both the prosperous and the poor about the future. What does Jesus teach by word and example about counting on God? In what sense are Jesus' word and example applicable equally to the prosperous and the poor?
- In pairs or threes hear responses to the question on study manual page 97, *What does the Jesus of Matthew 6 require of you?*

Going Forth (10 minutes)

- Preview Lesson 12. Hear prayer concerns.
- Pray in unison the prayer on study manual page 97.
- View Video Segment 11 Part II.

12 The Choice

Coming Together (30 minutes)

- Gather with prayer.
- Sing or read the words of a hymn.
  "O Day of God, Draw Nigh" or "I Know Whom I Have Believed"
- Prepare to view video.
  Presenter: Hyesung Hong Lee, Adjunct Professor in New Testament, Garrett-Evangelical Theological Seminary.
  Listen for how the reality of judgment is acknowledged and expressed in both Old and New Testaments and for Jesus' teachings on the relationship between discipleship and judgment.
- View Video Segment 12 Part I.
- Discuss after viewing:
  What is the connection between judgment and other biblical themes—sin? grace? love? forgiveness? hope? God's lordship over creation and history? How did Jesus' teaching bring together the concepts of the kingdom of God and the "day of the Lord" (final judgment)? How does belief in the Last Judgment shape and empower the life of disciples? How do Jesus' teachings both warn and assure his followers? How is the disciple's present connected with God's future?

Beginning With Moses and All the Prophets (45 minutes)

- Examine sayings about judgment. In groups of three or four focus first on Matthew 7:1-5 and Luke 6:37-42, using **GC 12-1** and study manual pages 100–101 in discussing these questions: How are these verses generally understood, quoted, and applied? How does knowing that the passages are addressed to the church and the practice of correcting one another affect your understanding? What new insights come with understanding that the "hypocrite" is the fellow disciple? What are the implications of understanding that the meaning here of *judge* is condemn and that "be judged" refers to God's judging at the Last Judgment? Now read the quotation in large type on study manual page 100 and respond to this question: What is the difference between condemning a person and making moral judgments about right and wrong?
- Consider the sayings on the narrow gate/hard road and the two houses. Ask the group to turn to **GC 12-2** and locate the placement of the sayings. Then in groups of three or four review Matthew 7:13-14 and Luke 13:23-24 and recall how Luke's point in the saying differs from Matthew's point. Next review Matthew 7:24-27 and Luke 6:47-49 and look for ways the parable of the two houses refers to other parts of the Sermon on the Mount. Now review the verses between the two sayings (Matthew 7:15-23; Luke 6:43-46) and talk together about how the flow of thought in the passages emphasizes choice and its consequences.

Discuss these questions: What are the gates, doors, roads that confront us with choices? What makes the easy road attractive? What causes you to nod in agreement when you read these sayings of Jesus about the road to life and the road to death?

- Examine the biblical roots of Jesus' teaching of the two ways: Deuteronomy 11:26-28; 30:15-20; Psalm 1; Tobit 4:14-19; Sirach 15:11-20. Form two groups and instruct the groups to watch for such words as *way, ways, choice, choose, life,* and *path*—how the words are used, the images they evoke, and their teaching—and to look for how the five strong beliefs behind the teaching of the two ways are expressed in these passages: (1) God gave humanity a clear choice, (2) we can choose, (3) we are responsible for the choice, (4) we can do what is chosen, (5) the consequences are clear and certain.

The Choice (45 minutes)

- Focus on how to distinguish the true prophet from the false. Again using **GC 12-2**, identify the differences between Matthew 7:15-20 and Luke 6:43-45 and respond to this question: What answer do these passages give to the question of how to tell the true prophet from the false prophet? Now in two groups see how the problem of false prophets has been addressed throughout Scripture: Group 1—Deuteronomy 18:15-22; Jeremiah 28; Acts 20:17-38; Group 2—Deuteronomy 18:15-22; Ezekiel 13:1-16; 1 John 4. Use these questions to guide study of the passages: What is the test of a true prophet? What different forms did false prophecy take? What characterized the false prophets? Look then at Matthew 7:21-23 to see how it fits in the overall passage. What is the warning in these verses and what is sobering about them?
- Using New Testament Scriptures for Day 4, explore the idea that making moral judgments is both necessary and dangerous. Divide the Scriptures between two groups: Group 1—Romans 2:1-24; Galatians 6:1-10; Group 2—Romans 12:14-21; 1 Thessalonians 5:1-22. What judgments are ours to make? What guidance is here for the judgments we must make? In what sense can making moral judgments be dangerous? What is the message in the claim that God shows no partiality in terms of judgment?
- Though both sermons assume the disciple can do as Jesus says, Scriptures for Day 5 recognize that Christians need help in being faithful. Assign one of those Scripture passages to each of three groups. Instruct the groups to study the assigned passage using these questions: How does the passage describe the difficulties and the choices that will come? What counsel, encouragement, and warnings here are meant to aid faithfulness?

Do You Want to Become His Disciples, Too? (20 minutes)

- In what sense is adhering to the demands of the two sermons a way of allowing ourselves to be judged by the teacher? Talk in the total group.
- In pairs hear each other's response to the question on study manual page 105, *What is difficult and demanding in the Jesus you hear in Matthew 7?*

Going Forth (10 minutes)

- Preview Lesson 13. Hear prayer concerns.
- Pray in unison the prayer on study manual page 105.
- View Video Segment 12 Part II.

13 Faith as Wonder

Coming Together (30 minutes)

- Gather with prayer.
- Sing or read the words of a hymn.
  Stanzas 1–3 of "How Firm a Foundation" or Stanza 1 of "Precious Lord, Take My Hand"
- Prepare to view video.
  Presenter: Beverly R. Gaventa, Professor of New Testament, Princeton Theological Seminary.
  Listen for what the nature miracles in the Gospels tell us about Jesus and about the kingdom of God.
- View Video Segment 13 Part I.
- Discuss after viewing:
  Why was it important for the Gospels to connect Jesus' nature miracles with similarly miraculous events in Israel's history? What do the nature miracles in the Gospels tell us about Jesus? about God? about God's kingdom? How has your imagination been enlarged by your reading of Jesus' nature miracles?

Beginning With Moses and All the Prophets (60 minutes)

- The assumption guiding this week's study is that the meaning of a story depends largely on how it is told. Explore the meanings in Jesus' nature miracles by working through the assigned Scriptures one day at a time.
  Day 1—Using **GC 13-1** and daily notes, hear in groups of three or four what persons discovered about similarities and differences in Mark's two stories of the feeding of the crowds. What does Mark say about Jesus and about his disciples by telling *two* feeding stories? Why is Mark 8:14-21 important for Mark as a whole? Why does Mark link the disciples' failure to understand with Jesus' greatest miracles?
  Day 2—Read aloud Job 38:1-11. Then in the total group discuss the biblical understanding of God's majesty and the majesty of "nature." What connections do you see between the Bible's view of nature as God's creation and Matthew's portrayal of Jesus' nature miracles?
  Day 3—Consider the result of Luke's omission of what Mark reports between Mark 6:45 and 8:27. First, scan Mark 6:45–8:27 to identify Jesus' teachings and actions, keeping in mind Luke omits them. Read aloud Mark 6:30-44, skipping 6:45–8:26, and concluding with 8:27-30. How does hearing Mark 6:30–8:30 read without those verses change the Gospel's picture of Jesus?
  Day 4—Consider the distinctiveness of John's accounts of Jesus' feeding the crowds and walking on the water. What is the significance of Exodus 16 and Isaiah 55 for understanding the meaning of Jesus' deeds in John 6:1-34? In Mark's account of the feeding (Mark 6:30-56), the

disciples do not understand; in John it is the fed people who do not understand (John 6:14-15). How does John's emphasis on the crowd's misunderstanding affect the Gospel's picture of Jesus? How does that emphasis affect the meaning of Jesus' nature miracles? In the total group now describe the distinctiveness of each Gospel's telling of the story of Jesus' feeding the crowds. What claim about Jesus' mission is each Evangelist making?

Day 5—Consider the difference between the view of signs in John and in the Synoptics. Begin by reading the first sentence under "Signs Denied and Signs Given" on study manual page 111.

(1) In groups of three or four hear what persons discovered by comparing the Scriptures in **GC 13-2**. Describe the difference in the ways Matthew and Luke explain the sign of Jonah. Invite persons to say what they wrote about Jesus' claim of being "greater than."

(2) Then compare Jesus' response to the Pharisees in Mark 8:11-12 with the passages in **GC 13-2**. How do these different explanations of signs all support Jesus' mission? How did Jesus' sayings about signs challenge the expectations of the Pharisees and the disciples?

(3) Summarize the Synoptics' view of signs in contrast to John's view. In what ways do Christians today still seek signs to confirm who Jesus is?

Faith as Wonder (30 minutes)

- Explore the Synoptic Gospel accounts of Jesus' stilling the storm and walking on the water. First, review the numbered paragraphs under "Meaning Missed" on study manual page 109. Then compare Mark 4:35-41 with Matthew 8:23-27 and Luke 8:22-25. What do the close similarities in the Synoptic accounts suggest about the meaning of the story? How do you think the Gospels' first readers understood the disciples' response, "Who then is this . . . ?"

- In two groups work with **GC 13-3**, daily notes, and study manual pages 110–111 to examine how Mark and Matthew tell the story of Jesus' walking on the water. How do the differences in the story affect how you see Jesus and the disciples?

- Compare the words Jesus speaks to his disciples while walking on the water (Mark 6:50; Matthew 14:27, 31) with what he says to them after stilling the storm (Mark 4:40; Matthew 8:26; Luke 8:25). What clues do Jesus' words give you to the different purposes of the two stories?

Do You Want to Become His Disciples, Too? (20 minutes)

- Recall these statements from "So Then" on study manual page 113: "The nature miracles preach the gospel," and "they are believers' stories." Discuss why you think none of these stories reports that persons came to faith in response to Jesus' miraculous acts. Then put yourself in the storm-tossed boat or imagine yourself distributing bread to the crowd. In pairs retell one of Jesus' nature miracles from that angle.

- Hear responses to the question on study manual page 113, *When you read the stories of the nature miracles, who is the Jesus you see?*

Going Forth (10 minutes)

- Preview Lesson 14. Hear prayer concerns.
- Pray in unison the prayer on study manual page 113.
- View Video Segment 13 Part II.

14 Destiny Disclosed

Coming Together (30 minutes)

- Gather with prayer.
- Sing or read the words of a hymn.
  "Christ, Upon the Mountain Peak" or "O Wondrous Sight! O Vision Fair"
- Prepare to view video.
  Presenter: Emerson B. Powery, Associate Professor of New Testament and Chair of the Department of Theology, Lee University.
  The focus here is on Jesus' identity and purpose. Listen for the contrast between first-century expectations for the messiah and the type of Messiah Jesus would be.
- View Video Segment 14 Part I.
- Discuss after viewing:
  How do you explain the difference between Peter's idea of the expected messiah and Jesus' idea of himself as Messiah? Why would Jews of the first century have been shocked by depictions of a suffering Messiah and a resurrected Son of Man? In speaking of his life as a ransom (Mark 10:45), what was Jesus saying about his purpose?

Beginning With Moses and All the Prophets (60 minutes)

- The word *destiny* appears here for the first time in a lesson title. It's a weighty word. Turn to the contents page to see that the word appears in four lesson titles. Work in two groups to consider key ideas on destiny from the study manual commentary: *(1) Destiny sees a person's present from the standpoint of the future. (2) God destines what is in store because God guides human affairs in accord with divine purpose. (3) People are responsible for their own actions even though God sets their destiny.* Discuss the meaning of these ideas and their impact on human beings and on daily living. Where in these statements does the weightiness of the concept of destiny come through?
- Instructions for **GC 14-1** lead the reader to observe how careful the Gospel writers were in putting their material together. Jesus was not asking Who do you think I am? out of the blue. Invite persons to say what they learned about the context of Jesus' question.
- Consider the relationship between Jesus' identity and his destiny. Referring to notes on Mark 8:27-33; Matthew 16:13-23; and Luke 9:18-22 and observations from **GC 14-1**, identify the sequence of events reported in each account. How do Matthew's and Luke's accounts differ from Mark's? What do the exchanges between Jesus and Peter (including Peter's answer to Jesus' question) in each account contribute to your understanding of Jesus' identity? Notice that in each Gospel account Jesus' prediction of his suffering, death, and being raised follows his command not to tell who he is. What significance do you see in the prediction and the command having been placed together?

- In the Passion predictions Jesus most often refers to himself as Son of Man. In groups of three or four review the note "The Son of Man" on study manual page 123, paying particular attention to the background of the expression and its emphasis on the humanness of human beings, Jesus' use of the expression, and John's distinctive use of the expression. Mark's Gospel implies that Jesus' destiny defines what it means to be the Son of Man rather than the title's defining who Jesus is. Discuss this question: What point do you think Mark is making?
- Consider the connection Jesus makes between what he said about his destiny and what he demands of his followers. In groups of three focus on the sayings on discipleship in Mark 8:34-38. Talk about the kind of life to which the follower is called in Mark 8:34, the consequences of avoiding a life of self-denial and consequences of withholding allegiance to Jesus in 8:35-38. Ask persons to say how they understand what it means to take up the cross. Read the statement on Jesus' understanding of cross-bearing on study manual page 121. What are the demands in this view of cross-bearing? Invite the group to respond to this question: What connection do you see between allowing Jesus' destiny to shape our own and the statement, "Who we are today works its way into who we will be tomorrow"?

Destiny Disclosed (30 minutes)

- Look now at the story of the Transfiguration for what it reveals about Jesus' identity and destiny. Consult notes from Day 3 reading of Mark 9:2-29 and Luke 9:28-43 and reading of "Jesus' Destiny Confirms His Identity" on study manual pages 118–119. Get the story in mind—setting, what happened, what was said and heard, the meaning in the allusions to Moses and Elijah, changes in Jesus and what they meant. Hear observations on what persons discovered in comparing what the voice said in the three Transfiguration stories and comparing what the voice said at the baptism with what the voice said at the Transfiguration **GC 14-3**. What is the significance of the inclusion of the words "listen to him" by the voice at the Transfiguration though those words are missing at the baptism? Finally discuss this question: What does Jesus' transfiguration convey about his identity and destiny?
- Turn to **GC 14-2**. First, say what each Gospel writer wanted to accent. Then discuss this question: How does Mark 9:1 serve as a link between Jesus' first Passion prediction and the Transfiguration?

Do You Want to Become His Disciples, Too? (20 minutes)

- In Peter's rebuke of Jesus we are confronted by Jesus' question, "Who do you say that I am?" What is offensive about a suffering Messiah? What do we want to avoid in the image of a suffering Messiah—the detail in the suffering? the reason for the suffering? something else?
- In groups of three or four hear persons' written responses to the question on study manual page 121, *How do you answer Jesus' question, "Who do you say that I am?"*

Going Forth (10 minutes)

- Preview Lesson 15. Hear prayer concerns.
- Pray in unison the prayer on study manual page 122.
- View Video Segment Part II.

15 Merciful Discipline

Coming Together (30 minutes)

- Gather with prayer.
- Sing or read the words of a hymn.
  "There's a Wideness in God's Mercy" or "Freely, Freely"
- Prepare to view video.
  Presenter: Frank Gulley, Jr., Professor Emeritus of Church History, Vanderbilt University Divinity School.
  Listen for what is said about Matthew's view of the church and the issues confronting the church addressed by Matthew 18.
- View Video Segment 15 Part I.
- Discuss after viewing:
  According to Matthew's Gospel, what are some essential characteristics of the church? In what ways do Jesus' teachings in Matthew 18 reflect Matthew's expectations of those who make up the church? Identify the issues agitating the faithful in Matthew's church and why they were so crucial to the health of Matthew's church.

Beginning With Moses and All the Prophets (60 minutes)

- Begin study of Jesus' teachings in Matthew 18 by forming groups of three or four to discuss similarities and differences in the three Gospel passages in **GC 15-1**. What does Jesus' use of a child to illustrate his teaching about the Kingdom say about (1) what the Kingdom is, (2) what the Kingdom is not, and (3) who may enter the Kingdom? How does the *context* of this passage in each Gospel affect your understanding of the *meaning* of Jesus' teaching in each Gospel? How does what Jesus says to the disciples indicate what each Gospel wants us to know about Jesus? about the disciples? What effect does Mark 9:38 (and Luke 9:49) have on the message of this passage?
- Form three groups to explore the theme of church/community discipline in the readings for Days 2 and 3. Group 1—Deuteronomy 19:15-21; Proverbs 24:29; 29:1; Ecclesiastes 7:5; Sirach 19:13-17; 28:1-7. Group 2—1 Corinthians 5; 6:1-8; and 2 Corinthians 2:1-11. Group 3— Matthew 18:15-35 and Luke 17:1-4. Have each group review notes and scan the passages to (1) summarize what is expected of the community, and (2) identify evidence of "merciful discipline." Then in the total group talk about the differences and similarities in the perspectives on church discipline voiced by Paul's letters, the Old Testament and Apocrypha, and the Gospels. What does the placement of Jesus' parable of the debtor (Matthew 18:23-35) right after his teaching on forgiveness (18:21-22) say about Matthew's view of church discipline? What does the requirement of repentance in Luke 17:4 but not in Matthew 18:21-22 say about the difference between Matthew's and Luke's views of

forgiveness? What does Jesus mean when he talks about binding and loosing (Matthew 18:18), and what are the implications of this teaching for the church's role in disciplining itself?

- In new groups of three or four using **GC 15-2**, hear insights about Jesus' teaching on divorce in the Synoptics. Locate Luke 16:18 and read the surrounding verses. Then discuss these questions: What clue does Luke give to understanding Jesus' teaching on divorce (Luke 16:18) by *not* setting it as a response to the Pharisees' question, as in Matthew and Mark? Why do you think Matthew and Mark include an episode involving Jesus and children immediately after a teaching on divorce (but Luke does not)? In the total group talk about differences and similarities in Paul's teaching on divorce and marriage and Jesus' teaching.
- Review the New Testament readings for Day 5. Why do you think the New Testament writers consider the discipline of individual believers so crucial to the well-being of the community of believers?

Merciful Discipline (30 minutes)

- Recall this statement from study manual page 126: "Matthew lets Jesus point out that a proper attitude is essential for any discussion of the internal life of the church." What Scriptures from the week's readings especially point to the importance of proper attitude?
- Focus on Matthew's use of two parables in Jesus' teaching on church discipline. (1) *The parable of the stray sheep* (Matthew 18:12-14)— Why does Matthew connect the parable of the stray sheep to Jesus' teaching on church discipline? How does the relationship between sheep and shepherd in Jesus' parable illustrate the responsibilities of the church in maintaining its own internal life (18:15-20)? (2) *The parable of the forgiven debtor* (18:23-35)— What does the relationship between the king and his indebted slave illustrate about the significance and difficulty of forgiveness for the church's internal life? What is Jesus' message (by way of Matthew) to the church in the harsh ending to the parable? How can the church hold in tension Jesus' instruction to forgive seventy-seven times and his parable of the forgiven debtor?

Do You Want to Become His Disciples, Too? (20 minutes)

- In pairs discuss why and in what ways people continue to seek a church without internal conflict. To what extent does your church follow the disciplining procedures outlined in Matthew 18? What keeps a church today from disciplining its members by these procedures?
- What makes Jesus' teaching on forgiveness so hard to carry out fully? What stumbling blocks to your faith do you encounter in church life? What stumbling blocks have you placed in the way of others' faith?
- In pairs hear responses to the question on study manual page 130, *What surprises you or shocks you about the Jesus who comes through this week's readings?*

Going Forth (10 minutes)

- Preview Lesson 16. Hear prayer concerns.
- Pray in unison the prayer on study manual page 130.
- View Video Segment 15 Part II.

16 The Journey Is the Way

Coming Together (30 minutes)

- Gather with prayer.
- Sing or read the words of a hymn.
  "I Want Jesus to Walk With Me" or "Close to Thee"
- Prepare to view video.
  Presenter: Justo L. González, retired ministerial member of the Rio Grande Conference of The United Methodist Church.
  Listen for what is unique to Luke's Gospel and for why Jesus "set his face" toward Jerusalem.
- View Video Segment 16 Part I.
- Discuss after viewing:
  What is the significance of Jerusalem for Jesus in Luke's Gospel? Why is it so important for Luke that Jesus "set his face" toward Jerusalem? How and why does Luke present Jesus' actions and teachings on the way to Jerusalem with a view to Jesus' passion and resurrection?

Beginning With Moses and All the Prophets (45 minutes)

- Explore the distinctive section of Luke (9:51–18:14) to get a sense of the variety of stories and teachings only Luke includes and to see in them the many-sided Jesus that Luke portrays. Begin by forming five groups. Assign each group one of the portions of daily readings from Luke: Group 1 (Luke 9:51–10:42); Group 2 (Luke 11–12); Group 3 (Luke 13–14); Group 4 (Luke 15–16); Group 5 (Luke 17:1–18:14). Instruct groups to scan the assigned Scriptures to identify passages in four categories: (1) Parables or stories Jesus tells, (2) teachings or sayings of Jesus, (3) actions Jesus takes (such as eating a meal), and (4) Jesus' interactions with others. After groups have identified passages in each category, provide these questions to guide discussion: What overall themes connect the passages in each category? In other words, how are Jesus' parables connected with his eating meals? How are Jesus' teachings connected with his interactions with Pharisees? with his disciples? with marginalized people? What does Luke want readers to know about Jesus in these chapters? What does the Jesus in these chapters want to convey about himself and his mission?
- Now in two or three groups discuss some of the questions raised by the things to look for in the daily assignments.
  (1) What does Luke's unique report of the mission of the seventy (10:1-20) add to your understanding of Jesus and his disciples in Luke?
  (2) What do you think Luke intended to communicate by combining various sayings of Jesus in 12:35-59, each containing a warning?
  (3) Comparing Luke 14:1-6 with Luke 13:15 and Matthew 12:11, how does the setting for Jesus' teaching affect the meaning of the teaching?

(4) How does noting that the stray sheep in Matthew 18:12 is the lost sheep in Luke 15:3-4 affect your understanding of each Gospel's emphasis in Jesus' teaching?

(5) What insights did you discover in comparing the persistent widow in Luke 18:1-8 and the persistent friend in 11:5-8?

The Journey Is the Way (45 minutes)

- Recall the study manual's observation that the disciples learn Jesus' way by hearing what he says and overhearing what he says to others. In groups of three or four consult notes made on the week's readings to discuss themes of Jesus' teaching on the way to Jerusalem.

  The cost of discipleship—How do the images Jesus uses define his teachings about the cost of discipleship? How do his hearers respond to what he says? How do you respond?

  The purpose of the sabbath—Why is Jesus' healing on the sabbath met with such opposition? How does Jesus justify his actions as appropriate on the sabbath?

  The dangers of wealth—What does Jesus say about the dangers of wealth for would-be followers? How would you summarize the similar message in Jesus' parable of the dishonest manager, in the parable of the rich man and Lazarus (Luke 16), and in his response to the rich ruler (18:18-30)? What response does Jesus' message receive in today's world? What is your response to it?

  The gospel as good news and bad news—Who hears Jesus' teaching about the Kingdom as bad news and why? Who hears Jesus' teaching about the Kingdom as good news and why? According to Jesus, what determines how we receive his message as bad news or good news?

- Turn to study manual page 141. Read the chart silently, recalling the passages from daily study. In the total group discuss what the material in this unique section of Luke adds to your picture of Jesus. What would be missing from Luke's portrayal of Jesus without this material?

Do You Want to Become His Disciples, Too? (20 minutes)

- The Jesus we see in Luke 9:51–18:14 sometimes warns and sometimes assures. Form two groups. Group 1—Scan the readings in Luke to identify six teachings of Jesus that *assure*. Group 2—Scan the readings in Luke to identify six teachings of Jesus that *warn*. Then come together to hear the six passages from each group read aloud, one at a time, alternating between Group 1 (assurances) and Group 2 (warnings). How do you respond to hearing these contrasting messages of Jesus?
- When in this week's reading did you find Jesus telling you what you *needed* to hear, not necessarily what you *wanted* to hear?
- What questions do you have of the Jesus in this week's readings?
- In pairs hear responses to the question on study manual page 140, *Who is this Jesus who determines the shape of your discipleship?*

Going Forth (10 minutes)

- Preview Lesson 17. Hear prayer concerns.
- Pray in unison the prayer on study manual page 140.
- View Video Segment 16 Part II.

17 Destiny Symbolized

Coming Together (30 minutes)

NOTES

- Gather with prayer.
- Sing or read the words of a hymn.
  "Hosanna, Loud Hosanna" or "All Glory, Laud, and Honor"
- Prepare to view video.
  Presenter: Dan P. Cole, Professor Emeritus of Religion and Mediterranean Archaeology, Lake Forest College.
  Listen for the role of the Temple, its structure, its development, and its importance in the lives of people in Jesus' day.
- View Video Segment 17 Part I.
- Discuss after viewing:
  What were expectations of devout Jews living in or near Jerusalem regarding the Temple? How did the expansive size of Herod's Temple contribute to (1) the dispelling of the Temple's aura of holiness in Jesus' day, and (2) the impact of Jesus' claim, "Destroy this temple, and in three days I will raise it up." How does awareness of the magnitude of the Temple and its place in Jewish life inform our understanding of Jesus' actions and teachings related to the Temple?

Beginning With Moses and All the Prophets (45 minutes)

- Call attention to the title of the lesson and in the total group establish the context for the lesson. Look at the title of Lesson 14 and recall what was disclosed about Jesus' destiny. Then discuss how Jesus' actions in Jerusalem symbolize his destiny.
- Mark's Gospel frames Jesus' action in the Temple with the story of the fig tree. In groups of three or four use **GC 17-G** and study manual page 146 to compare Mark's version of the story to Matthew's. Highlight differences and similarities in the two accounts. Also locate Matthew's version of the story in the Bible (Matthew 21:18-22) to see its setting. Then discuss these questions: What point does Jesus make by cursing the fig tree? In what ways do Mark's placement of the story and Matthew's placement of the story affect the point of the story? How do the passages from Jeremiah 7:1-15 and Isaiah 56:1-8 illuminate the meaning of the story? In what way might the message of Jesus' action in the Temple be different if Mark had left out the story of the fig tree?
- All four Gospel accounts of Jesus' entry into Jerusalem quote passages from the Old Testament (Zechariah 9:9-10; Psalm 118:26). What do the Gospel writers accomplish by doing this? Regarding Jesus' entry into Jerusalem, what do the Old Testament quotations reveal about (1) Jesus' understanding of what he is doing? (2) the crowd's understanding of what Jesus is doing? (3) the Gospel writer's understanding of what Jesus is doing?

50

- Make connections between the biblical view of true worship and Jesus' critique of what worship in the Temple had become. Hear in the total group summaries of what the Old Testament readings for Day 5 say true worship is. Then discuss this question: To what extent was Jesus' action in the Temple a continuation of the prophetic call for authentic worship or a call for a new form of worship? Read aloud the paragraph under "They Have No Wine." How does the church's worship lose its sense of the Holy One today? What actions are needed to bring about a correction?

Destiny Symbolized (45 minutes)

- Explore the distinctive elements in the four Gospel accounts of Jesus' entry into Jerusalem. Form new groups of three or four to hear what persons discovered by comparing the passages in **GC 17-1**. Refer to notes made each day on the things to look for. Then consider some of the people in the story—the bystanders, the crowds waving branches [in John], the Pharisees. For a few moments, imagine yourself as one of those people. What do you make of what you see? What do you make of Jesus? How would you explain what you experienced to someone who did not witness the event? What questions or feelings linger with you after the event is over? Invite persons to discuss responses to these questions within each group.
- In the total group describe your church's celebration of Palm Sunday—people involved, hymns sung, liturgy used. What message about Jesus' entry into Jerusalem does the church's celebration of Palm Sunday convey? How does that message compare to the message the Gospel writers convey?
- Again in groups of three or four explore the Gospel accounts of Jesus' action in the Temple, using **GC 17-2**. Pay particular attention to what is unique to each Gospel—for example, the detail in Mark 11:16, Jesus' healing in the Temple in Matthew 21:14, the observation in Luke 19:47, and the setting of the episode in John (John 2). How do these unique features signal what each Gospel writer wants to say about the event?

Do You Want to Become His Disciples, Too? (20 minutes)

- Imagine being a disciple with Jesus as he entered Jerusalem on a donkey and when he overturned tables in the Temple. You hear him curse a fig tree and later proclaim, "Have faith in God." In pairs talk about how you think the disciples reconciled these images of Jesus. Or did they?
- Of these two differing images of Jesus—riding humbly into Jerusalem and driving sellers out of the Temple—which one do you think the church holds up more often and why? Which one do you find easier to identify with and why?
- Hear responses to the suggestion on study manual page 150, *Describe the Jesus who confronts you both by riding into Jerusalem on a donkey and overturning tables in the Temple.*

Going Forth (10 minutes)

- Preview Lesson 18. Hear prayer concerns.
- Pray in unison the prayer on study manual page 151.
- View Video Segment 17 Part II.

18 Sharp Words in the Temple

Coming Together (30 minutes)

NOTES

- Gather with prayer.
- Sing or read the words of a hymn.
  "At the Name of Jesus" or "Majesty, Worship His Majesty"
- Prepare to view video.
  Presenter: John R. Levison, Professor of New Testament, Seattle Pacific University.
  Listen for Mark's and Matthew's perspectives on the confrontations between Jesus and the religious leaders.
- View Video Segment 18 Part I.
- Discuss after viewing:
    What issues were at stake in the Pharisees' questioning of Jesus? How does knowing that Jesus attacks Jewish leaders from the perspective of a Jewish rival help in understanding the meaning and purpose of his attacks? How are we to understand the tough indictments in Matthew 23?

Beginning With Moses and All the Prophets (45 minutes)

- Explore the variety of questions put to Jesus by various people in this week's Scriptures. Assign the three lists of passages from the chart on study manual page 163 to three groups and give these instructions: First, look up the passages to identify (1) who asked the question of Jesus, (2) what the question was, (3) what the purpose was in asking the question, (4) what Jesus' answer was and what form it took, and (5) what response Jesus' answer received. Then discuss these questions: What do these passages contribute to the Gospel writer's portrayal of those opposed to Jesus? of Jesus himself? How would the significance of these passages change if their setting were not the Temple?
- Form new groups to study Gospel portions using Gospel Comparisons. (1) Using **GC 18-1** and daily notes, discuss similarities and differences noted in the accounts of the parable of the vineyard. Consider these questions: What is the relationship between the message of Isaiah's song of the vineyard (Isaiah 5:1-7) and Jesus' parable? What effect does Matthew's pairing of the parable of the two sons with the parable of the vineyard have on the messages of both parables? Why do you think Luke shortened the quotation about the rejected stone? According to Matthew 21:43 who is deprived of the Kingdom and who receives it? (2) Explore each Gospel's depiction of Jesus in his response to the Sadducees' question about resurrection. Refer to **GC 18-2**, study manual page 159, and daily notes to discuss these questions: How does Luke's omission of Jesus' accusatory remark in Mark 12:24 change the way Jesus comes across? What meaning does Jesus' fuller response in Luke 20:34-36 add to what Mark and Matthew record? Both the Sadducees

and Jesus appeal to Torah to make their points—What does that say about the relationship between Jesus and his opponents? (3) Discuss similarities and differences noted in **GC 18-3**. Compare the subject and setting of the question and who asks it in each Gospel. What does Jesus' concluding remark convey about what he wants the questioner to understand? How does Luke 10:25-28 set the stage for the parable of the Good Samaritan?

Sharp Words in the Temple (45 minutes)

- In all three Synoptics the question of Jesus' authority is raised at the beginning of his Temple teaching. Form new groups to compare the passages in **GC 18-G**. Begin by reading the Scriptures cited on study manual page 156 (Mark 1:27; 2:10-11; 6:1-3; Matthew 12:38-39). Then discuss these questions: Why does Jesus appeal to John's authority in responding to a question about his own authority? What connection do you see between the issue of Jesus' authority and all the questions put to Jesus in the Temple? How do Jesus' responses to questions of authority serve each Gospel's purpose?

- In the total group compare the sharp words of Jesus in the Temple with the words of Old Testament prophets. Assign four people these Old Testament passages: Isaiah 3:16-26; Jeremiah 4:5-8; Jeremiah 15:6-7; and Amos 2:4-5. Assign another four people these Gospel passages: Mark 12:38-40; Matthew 23:23-24; Matthew 23:33-36; Luke 19:42-44. Hear the Old Testament passages read aloud first. Then hear the Gospel passages read aloud. How do Jesus' words of condemnation differ from the prophets' words in terms of tone and purpose?

- To understand the significance of the Temple setting in this week's Scriptures, imagine where Jesus might encounter similar questions in our day. How might the questions be phrased differently? What different shape might Jesus' responses take? Invite persons, individually, to paraphrase one of this week's passages from Mark, setting it in a contemporary context. Read carefully the passage to be sure the point of the question and the point of Jesus' response are conveyed accurately. Hear paraphrases in the total group. Then discuss this question: To what extent do the questions the world, the church, or you put to Jesus today relate to the issue of his authority?

Do You Want to Become His Disciples, Too? (20 minutes)

- Call attention to the five questions highlighting Mark 11:27–12:37 on study manual page 161. In pairs describe the basic theological issue believers still face in each question. When have you heard these issues raised in the "Temple," that is, in church life?

- What are your most urgent questions of Jesus at this time in your life of faith? How do you answer these questions: Whom shall we obey? and What may we hope for?

- In pairs hear responses to the question on study manual page 162, *Why is this Jesus decisive for you?*

Going Forth (10 minutes)

- Preview Lesson 19. Hear prayer concerns.
- Pray in unison the prayer on study manual page 162.
- View Video Segment 18 Part II.

19 Signs of Danger and Dangerous Signs

Coming Together (30 minutes)

- Gather with prayer.
- Sing or read the words of a hymn.
"Rejoice, the Lord Is King" or "Lo, He Comes With Clouds Descending"
- Prepare to view video.
Presenter: Osvaldo D. Vena, Associate Professor of New Testament Interpretation, Garrett-Evangelical Theological Seminary.
Listen for the development and purpose of apocalyptic literature and its connection to Jesus' teaching of the coming of God's kingdom.
- View Video Segment 19 Part I.
- Discuss after viewing:
What factors in Israel's history led to the development of apocalyptic writing? How is apocalyptic writing related to the promise of God's covenant in the Old Testament and to the coming of God's kingdom in the New Testament? What apocalyptic themes did Jesus' message include or reinterpret?

Beginning With Moses and All the Prophets (45 minutes)

- Explore the content of Jesus' discourse on the future in Mark 13 by working through the Scriptures for Days 1–4 one day at a time.
Day 1—Establish the source of biblical imagery depicting the future. Begin by hearing someone read aloud brief passages from the prophets: Amos 5:18-20; Isaiah 13:6-10; Ezekiel 7:2-4. Then turn to **GC 19-1** and read in unison Jesus' words in Mark 13:7-8. Form groups of three or four to consider the contrast between the setting of the prophets' words (addressed publicly to Israel) and the setting of Jesus' words (addressed privately to the disciples). How does the setting of Jesus' warnings affect their meaning? What does the disciples' question in each Gospel reveal about what they want to know about the future? Why is Jesus concerned about his disciples' being led astray?
Day 2—Read aloud Micah 7:5-6, followed by Mark 13:12-13. Identify the context of the Micah passage. What connection do you see between the prophet's judgment of Israel and Jesus' prediction of what his disciples will face?
Day 3—Identify the "desolating sacrilege" mentioned in Mark 13:14. Review information on study manual page 169. What did the Gospel writers want to convey in reporting Jesus' warning about the "desolating sacrilege"?
Day 4—(1) In the total group hear Isaiah 13:10 read aloud and identify its context. Then turn to **GC 19-2**. Compare what these events in the heavens signify for Isaiah and for the Gospels. How can Luke view these events as occasions of hope (Luke 21:28)? (2) Compare the lesson

of the fig tree in **GC 19-2** with Jesus' cursing of the fig tree in **GC 17-G**.
(3) Then talk about what concerns or issues facing early Christians
might have prompted the Gospel writers and Paul to urge their commu-
nities to keep awake. Why has that urging been necessary for succeeding
generations of Christians?

Signs of Danger and Dangerous Signs (45 minutes)

- Look now at what this week's readings imply for discipleship. Form
  three groups to scan the Gospel readings looking for Scriptures calling
  for adherence to Jesus in rough times (Group 1), faithfulness until the
  end of the age (Group 2), accountability in terms of obedience and
  righteousness (Group 3). In the total group hear groups summarize
  Jesus' message that disciples need to hear in the Scriptures they located.
  Why are the Scriptures in this lesson difficult to hear and to heed for
  many Christians? for you? Why do Mark 13, Matthew 24, and Luke 21
  all outline a sequence of future events but keep secret the exact time of
  the end of the age?
- Focus on the themes of preparedness and accountability in Luke 19:12-27
  and Matthew 25.
  (1) Begin with the parable of the ten bridesmaids in Matthew 25:1-13.
  According to the parable, what constitutes being prepared for the coming
  of the Kingdom? What are the consequences of being unprepared? What
  does Luke 12:35-36 add to the parable's call to preparedness?
  (2) Turn to **GC 19-3**. Discuss the similarities and differences in
  Matthew's parable of the talents and Luke's parable of the pounds.
  What is Luke's purpose in introducing the subplot and how does it
  affect the meaning of the parable? What does each parable teach about
  preparedness and accountability in light of the coming Kingdom?
  What message do you hear in the harsh ending to each parable? How
  does Matthew's parable of the talents (25:14-30) prepare you for
  understanding the Last Judgment (25:31-46)? What does seeing the
  needy recipient of deeds of mercy as judge in the end, contribute to
  your understanding of Jesus' teachings in this week's readings?

Do You Want to Become His Disciples, Too? (20 minutes)

- Imagine your own child or a close friend or another loved one is going
  to a dangerous place—a place where her faith and perhaps her life will
  be threatened. As a fellow believer, reflect on the teachings of Jesus in
  this week's Scriptures and write a note of warning and encouragement
  to this person. Hear what persons wrote.
- In pairs talk about the extent to which the Jesus who emerges from this
  week's readings is unfamiliar or unattractive and why.
- Hear responses to the question on study manual page 174, *What is it
  about Jesus as judge that calls you to be obedient in the present and
  unafraid of the future?*

Going Forth (10 minutes)

- Preview Lesson 20. Hear prayer concerns.
- Pray in unison the prayer on study manual page 175.
- View Video Segment 19 Part II.

20 Destiny Seized

Coming Together (30 minutes)

- Gather with prayer.
- Sing or read the words of a hymn.
  Stanza 1 of "Go to Dark Gethsemane" or "Bread of the World"
- Prepare to view video.
  Presenter: L. Gregory Jones, Dean and Professor of Theology, Duke University Divinity School.
  Listen for how the Passover meal and the symbol of the cup draw together the past, present, and future of God's story of redemptive love.
- View Video Segment 20 Part I.
- Discuss after viewing:
  What images do the Gospel writers use to connect God's covenant with Israel and God's redemptive purpose through Jesus? Say what the images mean. What does Jesus' acceptance of the cup accomplish? Why is the meal with the cup pivotal and decisive for our salvation?

Beginning With Moses and All the Prophets (45 minutes)

- Call attention to the title of the lesson and in the total group establish the context for the lesson. Look at the title of Lesson 14 and recall what was disclosed about Jesus' destiny. Then talk about how this lesson's beginning study of the Passion story shows Jesus seizing that destiny. Recall the glossary definition of *Passion Story*. Turn to **GC 14-4** and read the first Passion prediction in the three Gospel accounts, paying attention to the word *must*. Discuss this question: What does it mean to say that the word *must* establishes the perspective of the Passion story?
- Consider how each Gospel invites readers to "see into" the events in the Passion story. Form three groups with each group considering one day's assigned Scriptures and suggestions of things to look for: Group 1, Day 1; Group 2, Day 2; Group 3, Day 3. Instruct the groups to discuss their observations of how the Gospel writer told the story, to identify details that helped them "see into" what was happening in the story, and to say what crucial information the assigned non-Gospel passages bring to their understanding of the assigned Gospel.
- Keeping the Synoptic Gospel accounts in mind, form two groups to see how John's accounts clarify the Synoptic accounts: Group 1, Day 4; Group 2, Day 5.

Destiny Seized (45 minutes)

- The story of Jesus' passion is also the story of people who are remembered. Consider three: the anointer, the betrayer, the denier. Use these questions to guide study and discussion of how these persons are remembered: What role did each play in Jesus' passion? How did Jesus respond to each of them? When you hear them mentioned, what comes to mind? Work in groups of three or four. Trace mentions of each person through the Synoptic Gospel accounts using **GC 20-1** and through John using the Bible. Review the commentary on study manual pages 180–181 and 183–184.

■ Jesus, the self-giver, is the most remembered person in the Passion story. Recall that in Mark 10:45 Jesus interprets the purpose of his mission as service—his life a ransom for many. As a total group work through the many dimensions of the preparation and the meal to arrive at Jesus' restatement of the meaning of his death:

(1) Hear the Gospel accounts of Passover preparation read aloud from **GC 20-1**.

(2) Clarify understanding of what the last meal is called. Review "The Names of the Last Meal" on study manual page 179. Why do the Synoptics call the meal "Passover"?

(3) Study the "words of institution" from the ritual Jesus institutes at the meal. Review the variations in the wording of the formulation on study manual page 182. Discuss these questions: What is the relationship between Jesus' actions and his words in the ritual? What is your understanding of why the actions and the words must never be separated?

(4) Turn to **GC 20-G** and hear the three accounts read aloud. Then review "Luke's Account of the Supper," on study manual page 187. Use **GC 20-1** to make the comparisons mentioned in this note. Discuss these questions: How do Jesus' actions enact the meaning of his death? What action of the disciples made them participants in the meaning of Jesus' death?

(5) The cup saying in the three Synoptic accounts refers to the covenant differently. Read the cup sayings in **GC 20-G**. Discuss these questions: What words and images from covenant-making between God and Israel in the Old Testament did Jesus draw on in his saying about cup and covenant? How then did Jesus restate the meaning of his death at this meal?

■ To get a sense of the Gospels' varying perceptions of Jesus in the Passion story thus far, move quickly through the Synoptic accounts and John's account guided by the chart on study manual page 176. Use **GC 20-1** and Bibles for the John passages. Look for events that show Jesus in charge, events where Jesus is acted upon, evidence of the Passion story as the working out of what Jesus had foreseen, evidence that the Passion story is about Jesus and God at the same time.

Do You Want to Become His Disciples, Too? (20 minutes)

■ Read aloud Mark 14:36 from study manual page 176. Discuss these questions: How does Jesus' Gethsemane prayer confront the disciple? How is Jesus' agony in the garden good news for the disciple who is resisting God's will?

■ In the total group hear each person's response to the suggestion on study manual page 187, *Picture Jesus at each event in the Passion story and then describe the whole Jesus you see.*

Going Forth (10 minutes)

■ Preview Lesson 21. Hear prayer concerns.
■ Pray in unison the prayer on study manual page 187.
■ View Video Segment 20 Part II.

21 Destiny Achieved

Coming Together (30 minutes)

- Gather with prayer.
- Sing or read the words of a hymn.
  "O Sacred Head, Now Wounded" or "Were You There"
- Prepare to view video.
  Presenter: Peter J. Storey, Professor of the Practice of Christian Ministry, Duke University Divinity School.
  Listen for how Jesus' death on the cross relates to his love and faithfulness.
- View Video Segment 21 Part I.
- Discuss after viewing:
  What was the purpose of crucifixions in Palestine of Jesus' day? What was the purpose of Jesus' crucifixion? How did Jesus challenge both religious and political authorities? In what way was Jesus' death on the cross inevitable? What is the connection between Jesus' death on the cross and his identity?

Beginning With Moses and All the Prophets (45 minutes)

- The word *destiny* appears for the final time in a lesson title. Recall the disciples' difficulty in understanding Jesus' predictions of his destiny by turning to **GC 14-4** and reading aloud Mark 8:31; Matthew 17:22-23; and Luke 18:31-34. How do the Gospels portray the disciples' understanding of Jesus' destiny *achieved*? How are Jesus' passion predictions important for our understanding of Jesus' destiny achieved?
- Using **GC 21-1**, the chart on study manual page 188, and daily notes, explore in groups of three or four what the Gospels say about Jesus' last hours. Consider Mark 15 the starting point and discuss how Matthew, Luke, and John modify, add to, or omit what Mark reports about Jesus' passion. Pay attention to what passages are unique to each Gospel and discuss why you think they are included. In particular (1) identify the titles used to describe Jesus in each Gospel—Who uses them and what role do they play in the Passion story? and (2) identify the last words Jesus speaks in each Gospel—What do they disclose about how the Gospel writer wants the reader to view Jesus in his dying?
- Compare the Gospels' portrayal of Pilate and his role in the Passion story. Still using **GC 21-1** and recalling the commentary on study manual pages 193–194, discuss these questions: Of what importance is Pilate to each Gospel's telling of the story of Jesus' last hours? Of what importance is Pilate to each Gospel's depiction of the Jewish authorities opposed to Jesus? Call attention to the note "Pontius Pilate" on study manual page 192 and read the last sentence. How do you regard Pilate—as a villain? a saint? what?

- Compare early preaching about the Passion with the Gospel accounts. Form four groups. Assign to each group one of the following preachers in the Day 4 readings: Peter (Acts 3:11-21), Stephen (Acts 7:51-60), Philip (Acts 8:26-35), and Paul (Acts 13:23-31). Have groups scan the preachers' sermons for context and content with this question in mind: How is the message proclaimed about Jesus' passion in early preaching like or unlike the message proclaimed in the Gospel stories?

Destiny Achieved (45 minutes)

- Recall that because the Gospel writers do not give us all the details of Jesus' final hours, we are not distracted by matters that only satisfy our curiosity. Form new groups of three or four to consider some of the details of Jesus' passion the Gospels do give us.
  (1) First, review the passages in each Gospel referring to Jesus' suffering and crucifixion. Based on those Scriptures alone, form a mental picture of what you would have seen had you been there. Do this with each Gospel, one at a time, jotting down what you can see and what you cannot see. What effect does the Gospels' lack of detail in telling the events of Jesus' suffering and death have on the way you picture the scene? What is your response to the scene you picture?
  (2) Scan study manual pages 194–197 and locate all the references to passages from the noncanonical *Gospel of Peter* and *Gospel of the Nazaraeans*. What details of information or insight do these passages add to the Gospel accounts of Jesus' passion? Then discuss this question: If we did have more information about Jesus' passion, would we find it easier to become his followers? Why or why not?
  (3) Consider several main figures in the Passion story who make only brief appearances in more than one Gospel. Using **GC 21-1** again, read the passages that mention (1) Simon of Cyrene; (2) the centurion; (3) Joseph of Arimathea; and (4) the women, named and unnamed, who witness the Crucifixion. Why are these people important enough to be included in the Gospel accounts? How would their absence affect the meaning of Jesus' passion? As a result of their experience of Jesus' crucifixion, what do you think they understood about Jesus?

Do You Want to Become His Disciples, Too? (20 minutes)

- In what ways do the experiences in your life influence how you read the Passion story, particularly at this time?
- Having studied the story of Jesus' crucifixion, how do you understand Jesus' call to take up your cross and follow him?
- Call attention to the statement on study manual page 198 that the Gospels alert us to the uncomfortable fact that the same realities that animated those hostile to Jesus also animate us. When has that been true for you?
- In pairs hear responses to the question on study manual page 199, *Why is this crucified Jesus the one you look for and want to follow?*

Going Forth (10 minutes)

- Preview Lesson 22. Hear prayer concerns.
- Pray in unison the prayer on study manual page 199.
- View Video Segment 21 Part II.

22 This Jesus God Raised Up

Coming Together (30 minutes)

NOTES

- Gather with prayer.
- Sing or read the words of a hymn.
  "Christ the Lord Is Risen Today" or "Lord of the Dance"
- Prepare to view video.
  Presenter: Ellen T. Charry, Associate Professor of Systematic Theology, Princeton Theological Seminary.
  Listen for what Jesus' resurrection says about God and what it means for us as believers.
- View Video Segment 22 Part I.
- Discuss after viewing:
  How was Jesus' resurrection unlike other examples of raising the dead in Scripture? What does it mean to say that the Incarnation, the Crucifixion, and the Resurrection are "the complement of events in the life of God that constitute the mission of the Son of God in the world"? How does God use the Resurrection to get our attention and what does the Resurrection mean for our lives?

Beginning With Moses and All the Prophets (45 minutes)

- This lesson's assumption is that without the Resurrection there would be no Christian faith. Clarify the concept of resurrection and the language used to express it. In the total group hear 1 Corinthians 15:3-8 read aloud. Next, individually, scan Scriptures and review daily notes for Day 1 to identify the points Paul makes about Jesus' resurrection. Refer also to study manual page 205. Then in groups of three or four respond to these questions: According to Paul, why is the Resurrection central to the good news of Jesus? Where in Paul's letters do you see support for the claim that what is really at stake in resurrection is the nature and power of God? Consider Paul's meaning in the resurrection metaphor of "first fruits" (1 Corinthians 15:20): What other image might express a similar insight about the concept of resurrection?
- Compare the four Gospel accounts of Jesus' resurrection, making use of **GC 22-1**. Form three groups, assigning each group a portion of all four Gospel passages: Group 1—the empty tomb (highlighted in yellow); Group 2—the post-Resurrection appearances; Group 3—the Ascension and/or commissioning. In each group discuss the similarities and differences persons discovered in comparing the four passages. Refer to daily notes made in response to the things to look for in Days 2–5. Then discuss this question: What truth about Jesus' resurrection does each Gospel writer express through this portion of the story? Then in the total group hear responses to this question: According to the Gospels, why is the Resurrection central to the good news of Jesus?

60

This Jesus God Raised Up (45 minutes)

- Following the organization of the commentary on study manual pages 204–209, examine the Gospels' Easter logic.
  (1) *Resurrection logic.* Describe the connection between the Gospel stories of Jesus' resurrection and the vision of resurrection recorded in Daniel 12:1-3. Why is the distinction between resuscitation and resurrection so important to make in understanding the first Easter? Where do you see evidence today of the Sadducees' misunderstanding of the concept of resurrection—*status quo ante*?
  (2) *Appearance logic.* Briefly identify the five things *not* found in the appearance stories in the Gospels and in Paul (study manual page 206). Which of the five things helps you most appreciate what the Scriptures do say about Jesus' post-Resurrection appearances? Which of Jesus' appearances—to Mary Magdalene, to the disciples, to the two at Emmaus, to Thomas—leaves you most able to confirm, "God raised Jesus from the dead"?
  (3) *Concluding logic.* Turn again to **GC 22-1** to recall how each Gospel concludes. Then discuss each Gospel writer's emphasis one at a time.
  Mark—Use notes made in response to the things to look for in suggestion (6) under Day 5 to talk about how the additions to Mark (16:9-20) change the impact of the shorter ending (16:1-8). Which of the two endings of Mark do you think is most consistent with the Gospel's purpose? Assuming Mark does end with 16:8, what response do you think the Gospel intended readers to make?
  Matthew—What is the significance of Matthew's setting the concluding scene on a mountain? How do Jesus' words in 28:20 convey the character and content of Matthew's Gospel? What response do you think Matthew intended his readers to make at the end of his Gospel?
  Luke—What meaning does Jesus' appearance to the disciples on the road to Emmaus add to Luke's conclusion? How does Jesus' being recognized in "the breaking of the bread" fit with the overall message of Luke? What response do you think Luke intended his readers to make at the end of his Gospel?
  John—What does Thomas's expression of doubt and ultimate confession of Jesus as Lord say about the intent of John's Gospel? Why doesn't John report the Ascension, even though Jesus often predicts it (John 14:2, 3, 28; 16:5-11, 28; 20:17)?

Do You Want to Become His Disciples, Too? (20 minutes)

- Read aloud the paragraph under "They Have No Wine" on study manual page 200. Then call attention to the paragraphs on page 209 that mention the words *grace* and *prevenient grace*. Keeping those two concepts in mind, discuss in pairs how you experience the risen Jesus.
- How has the transformed Jesus effected change in someone's life because of a change he made in your life?
- In pairs hear responses to the question on study manual page 210, *How does this resurrected Jesus reveal to you the purpose and power of God?*

Going Forth (10 minutes)

- Preview Lesson 23. Hear prayer concerns.
- Pray in unison the prayer on study manual page 210.
- View Video Segment 22 Part II.

23 In the Beginning Was the Word

Coming Together (30 minutes)

- Gather with prayer.
- Sing or read the words of a hymn.
  Stanzas 1, 2, and 4 of "Word of God, Come Down on Earth" or "Of the Father's Love Begotten"
- Prepare to view video.
  Presenter: Gail R. O'Day, A. H. Shatford Professor of New Testament and Preaching, Candler School of Theology.
  Listen for how the Gospel of John tells the beginning of the Jesus story, for the meaning of *the Word* in Genesis and in John, and for the centrality of the Incarnation in John's Jesus story.
- View Video Segment 23 Part I.
- Discuss after viewing:
  What connections does John want his readers to make between Jesus' story and the Creation story in Genesis? What is the relationship between God and the Word? What is the role of the Word? Why is John's story of Jesus a story of God? What is your understanding of the Incarnation? of Jesus as the incarnate Word?

Beginning With Moses and All the Prophets (45 minutes)

- Explore the relation of Christ to Creation emphasized at the beginning of John's Gospel. In groups of four using study notes on Scriptures for Day 1, review John 1:1-5; 1 Corinthians 8:4-6; Colossians 1:15-20; Hebrews 1:1-4. Discuss this question in relation to each passage: How does the passage describe the relation of Christ to Creation? Then talk together about insights gained from suggestions (2) through (5) under Day 1. Next work together to combine the ideas and images in Colossians 1:15-20 and Hebrews 1:1-4 in a litany or a paraphrase. Identify ideas about and images of Christ in the two passages and decide whether to write a paraphrase or a litany. Hear what each group has written.
- Examine biblical passages that serve as background for New Testament teachings on the relation of Christ and Creation. Begin by hearing Genesis 1:1–2:3 read aloud, with one person reading the part of narrator and the other reading God's words. Talk together about this question: From John's perspective, what does this passage from Genesis tell us about the relation of Christ and Creation? Now in groups of three or four review Proverbs 8:1-31; Wisdom of Solomon 7:22–8:1; Sirach 24:1-29 using these questions: How is wisdom described here? What is her relationship to God? How does she describe her role in Creation? How do these passages celebrate wisdom's role in Creation?
- John's report of how Jesus acquired his first disciples differs considerably from the reports in the Synoptics. In pairs or threes using **GC 23-1** and

"The Promise of Jesus" on study manual page 218, identify differences in those accounts. What does Jesus' promise to Nathanael (John 1:51) reveal about Jesus' mission?

- The idea that the Creator is also Redeemer appears in Old and New Testaments. In the total group look at Isaiah 40; 42:5-8; and John 1:1-18. Where do the Isaiah passages indicate that the Redeemer is the Creator? How does the John passage insist that the Redeemer is the Creator?

In the Beginning Was the Word (45 minutes)

- Begin consideration of John's Prologue with the identity of the Word. Hear John 1:1-5 read aloud. Then in the total group review "What John Meant by 'the Word' " on study manual page 221. Identify key ideas, define *Word*, define *Logos*, and get some sense of the Greek and Jewish thought behind *Logos*. Review the glossary definition of *Incarnation* on study manual page 298. With that background, discuss this question: Who is the Word according to John?

- Now hear John 1:1-18 read aloud. Invite groups of four to study the passage and respond to these questions: According to the Prologue whom is the story of Jesus about? What are we to expect in the story of Jesus? Why is Jesus so important? Next read John 1:1-18 silently and together write a statement that describes the perspective from which this Gospel tells the Jesus story. Hear each group's statement.

- Scriptures for Day 5 respond to false teaching about Jesus. In groups of four or six begin by reading John 1:14 and then, using daily study notes, talk about how the author of First and Second John responds to those who deny Jesus has come "in the flesh." Discuss what the words *light* and *darkness* are meant to convey here and in the Prologue.

- Look now at how the Gospel of John presents John the Baptizer. Invite groups of three or four to refer to Scripture and daily notes for Day 3 and "The Baptizer's Witness" on study manual page 217 to identify (1) all of John's self-descriptions (who he said he was), (2) John's descriptions of Jesus (who he said Jesus was), (3) Jesus' description of John the Baptizer (who the two of them were). Now hear what persons learned in their use of GC 23-2 in daily study. How does the Gospel of John subordinate the Baptizer more strongly than do the Synoptics? Then hear what persons observed and noted in their use of GC 23-3 regarding John's response to Jesus' popularity. Why is John not jealous of Jesus' popularity? Why do you think John the Baptizer is so confident that he knows who Jesus is and why Jesus is decisive for humankind?

Do You Want to Become His Disciples, Too? (20 minutes)

- Hear "They Have No Wine" read aloud. Now in the total group respond to this point: "The disciple is one who sees who Jesus is and accepts what he gives. And that is more than we are looking for."

- In twos or threes hear responses to the question on study manual page 219, *How does Jesus as the Word broaden, challenge, or confirm your understanding of who Jesus is?*

Going Forth (10 minutes)

- Preview Lesson 24. Hear prayer concerns.
- Pray in unison the prayer on study manual page 220.
- View Video Segment 23 Part II.

24 We Have Seen His Glory

Coming Together (30 minutes)

- Gather with prayer.
- Sing or read the words of a hymn.
  "This Is a Day of New Beginnings" or "Morning Has Broken"
- Prepare to view video.
  Presenter: R. Alan Culpepper, Founding Dean of the McAfee School of Theology, Mercer University.
  Listen for Jesus in the role of life-giver in John 2–4 and for Jesus as the fulfillment of Israel's hopes.
- View Video Segment 24 Part I.
- Discuss after viewing:
  What is the life Jesus gives in each of the five stories? What is John's concept of eternal life? How does the conversation between the Samaritan woman and Jesus overcome the barriers of gender, nationality, and religion? Where in these stories do you see Jesus as the fulfillment of Israel's hopes?

Beginning With Moses and All the Prophets (30 minutes)

- Focus on what Jesus' signs in the Gospel of John signify about Jesus. Consider the sign in Cana (John 2:1-12). In groups of three or four review Scripture and daily notes to identify the occasion for the story, participants in the story, words and actions of the participants, results of the actions, and responses to what happened. Now, drawing on "Signs Done and Signs Spoken" on study manual pages 226–227, talk about the meaning of the wedding metaphor, the significance of the six water jars, and of the good wine being kept until last. Observe the link between John 2:11 and 1:14. What does the word *glory* in these verses mean? How did Jesus reveal his glory in the sign in Cana? How did Jesus' turning water into wine at the beginning of his story foreshadow the significance of his death at the end? What does Jesus' sign in Cana signify about Jesus?
- In the same groups of three or four concentrate on the story of Jesus' action in the Temple. Compare John 2:13-22 with Mark 11:15-19 to identify distinctive features of John's story of Jesus in the Temple. How does Jesus' response to the request for a sign (John 2:19) illustrate the way Jesus uses words in the Gospel of John? What is the significance in the fact that Jesus' sign in Cana and his action in the Temple both have to do with Jewish religious practices?
- Compare various requests for a sign. In pairs using **GC 24-1**, talk first about what light the context for each passage throws on the passage. Then hear what each discovered in making the comparisons called for.

We Have Seen His Glory (60 minutes)

- Hear and understand two conversations—Jesus' conversation with Nicodemus and Jesus' conversation with the Samaritan woman. Study the stories one at a time starting with Jesus' conversation with Nicodemus. Form two groups and make these assignments: Group 1 will study John 3:1-21 and prepare to tell the story. Group 2 will study the commentary on Jesus and Nicodemus on study manual pages 227–228 and prepare to interpret what is said and done in the story and to explain what the story means. In the total group hear Group 1 tell the story and then, without comment, hear Group 2 explain what the story is saying. For the conversation between Jesus and the woman of Samaria, switch assignments. Group 2 will study John 4:1-42 and prepare to tell the story. Group 1 will study the commentary on Jesus and the Samaritan woman on study manual pages 228–229 and prepare to interpret what is said and done in the story and to explain what the story means. In the total group hear Group 2 tell the story and then, without comment, hear Group 1 explain the meaning in the story. Now discuss this question: What words did Jesus use that Nicodemus and the Samaritan woman heard but did not hear what the words conveyed? How are such words of Jesus like signs? Invite persons to talk about what they learned through looking at the stories in this way.
- In pairs use **GC 24-2** to explore the theme of seeing and believing. Talk about similarities discovered in the two passages during daily study. How is believing manifested in these stories? Pay attention to the exchanges between Jesus and the official and Jesus and the centurion. What do you learn from Jesus' words and the men's responses about seeing and believing? Now read John 20:29 on study manual page 222. Then review John 20:24-31 to see how seeing and believing in this story differs from the two previous stories. What is the implication for us in Jesus' response to Thomas?
- Teachings in John 2–4 alert the reader to themes that are important to the rest of John's Gospel. Form three groups and assign each group one chapter: Group 1—John 2; Group 2—John 3; Group 3—John 4. Instruct the groups to identify themes in these chapters important to the rest of the Gospel. Then discuss this question: What do these chapters convey about Jesus' mission?
- In the total group recall something of how the Synoptic Gospels reported what Jesus said and did. Then identify differences in the way John reports Jesus' words and actions.

Do You Want to Become His Disciples, Too? (20 minutes)

- The gospel John offers is this: *By believing in Jesus we begin all over again, repeatedly.* Talk in pairs about how that gospel is a sign of hope.
- In groups of three or four hear the written descriptions called for on study manual page 231, *Describe the Jesus you encountered through his signs.*

Going Forth (10 minutes)

- Preview Lesson 25. Hear prayer concerns.
- Pray in unison the prayer on study manual page 231.
- View Video Segment 24 Part II.

25 In Him Was Life

Coming Together (30 minutes)

- Gather with prayer.
- Sing or read the words of a hymn.
  "Fill My Cup, Lord" or "Break Thou the Bread of Life"
- Prepare to view video.
  Presenter: Jaime Clark-Soles, Assistant Professor of New Testament, Perkins School of Theology, Southern Methodist University.
  Listen for why understanding the Son-Father relationship between Jesus and God is key to understanding John's message.
- View Video Segment 25 Part I.
- Discuss after viewing:
  How does Jesus speak about his relationship with God to define his origin, mission, and authority? What does Jesus' relationship to God enable him to accomplish? How does Jesus' teaching about eternal life depend on his teaching about God as his Father?

Beginning With Moses and All the Prophets (45 minutes)

- Central to John 5–7 is how Jesus' mission takes shape through the issues it raises and the opposition it provokes. Look for clues to Jesus' mission by working through the three chapters one by one.
  John 5—Hear John 3:31-35 read aloud, followed by 5:19-20. What is Jesus saying about the source of his words and deeds? Why is it crucial for John's Gospel that Jesus clarify the nature of his relation to God? Consider Jesus' healing of the lame man: How does this healing show God "is still working"? In light of Genesis 2:2-3 (when God rested on the sabbath), what is the implication of Jesus' claim in 5:17 that God works on the sabbath? Now consider Jesus' discourse in 5:19-47: How do Jesus' two views of "life"—eternal life (5:24) and life after death (5:28-29)—express Jesus' mission? Why are Jesus' opponents "astonished" at his teaching?
  John 6—John's account of Jesus' feeding of the multitude and discourse on the bread of life alludes to the Exodus and to the Eucharist. Form two groups to discuss the implications of those allusions: Group 1 (the Exodus)—Exodus 16; Psalm 78:17-32; Group 2 (the Eucharist)—1 Corinthians 10:1-13. In each group review the assigned passage(s), study manual pages 237–238, and daily notes to respond to these questions: What meaning do the allusions give to Jesus' claim to be the "bread of life"? What part do the allusions play in provoking the complaints of the Jews (6:41) and the disciples (6:61)? What issues do the allusions raise for our understanding of Jesus' mission?
  John 7—Jesus' teachings continue to generate conflict. Still in two groups work through notes persons made on the things to look for listed

NOTES

under Day 5. Use these questions to guide discussion: How does the question about the source of Jesus' teaching in John 7:15 compare in tone to similar questions in Mark 6:2-3 and Luke 4:22? What do the question in John 7:15 and Jesus' response say about the issue of Jesus' authority? How is the issue of the Messiah's origin (7:25-31) related to the issue of Jesus' authority? How is Jesus' offer in 7:37-38 the answer to the question of his messiahship? What does John reveal *about* Jesus through what others say *against* him?

In Him Was Life (45 minutes)

■ Consider what Jesus says in John 5–7 to disclose himself as the "life-giver." Begin by hearing John 1:1-4, 10-13 read aloud. Then individually, scan the three chapters to identify passages where the word *life* appears. Next, review "The Words of the Word" on study manual pages 235–236 and discuss these questions: How does what John's Prologue says about Jesus help make sense of what Jesus says about himself? What do Jesus' words about the life he offers say about God? about Jesus' mission? about the expectations of those who receive it? about the fate of those who reject it?

■ Again individually, scan John 5–7, this time to identify what Jesus says about his relation to God. Pay attention to 5:19-29 and the itemized paraphrase of that passage on study manual page 236. Then discuss these questions: Why do Jesus' teachings about his relation to God cause controversy among the Jews in John? Why are those teachings important to John's portrayal of Jesus? In what way do those teachings continue to cause controversy among Christians today?

■ Call attention to the statement on study manual page 239: "When metaphors are effective, they make us think about the subject matter in fresh ways." What fresh understanding of Jesus did the crowds get from hearing his discourse on bread? What fresh understanding did the disciples get? do you get? Turn to the note, "The 'I Am' Sayings of Jesus" on study manual page 241 and skim the first paragraph. Then in pairs describe (1) the hungers Jesus the bread of life still satisfies and (2) what causes some still to be shocked by that metaphor.

Do You Want to Become His Disciples, Too? (20 minutes)

■ Reread the examples of Jesus' use of the present tense listed under "So Then" on study manual page 239. Form new pairs to talk about what it means to be sustained daily by Jesus' "present-tense" self-giving.

■ In John 6:60-68 Jesus asks his disciples whether his teaching offends them. How would you answer that question? When have you experienced Jesus' words as offensive or uncomfortable? Would you agree that being offended by Jesus' words at times is essential to your discipleship? Why or why not?

■ In pairs hear responses to the questions on study manual page 240, *What do Jesus' claims about himself reveal to you about his relationship to God? What response do his claims require of you?*

Going Forth (10 minutes)

■ Preview Lesson 26. Hear prayer concerns.
■ Pray in unison the prayer on study manual page 241.
■ View Video Segment 25 Part II.

67

26 Yet the World Did Not Know Him

Coming Together (30 minutes)

NOTES

- Gather with prayer.
- Sing or read the words of a hymn.
  "Jesus, Joy of Our Desiring" or "Christ Is the World's Light"
- Prepare to view video:
  Presenter: Robert D. Kysar, Bandy Professor Emeritus of Preaching and New Testament, Candler School of Theology, Emory University. Listen for the meanings of *light* and *darkness* in John's Gospel.
- View Video Segment 26 Part I.
- Discuss after viewing:
  Identify the meanings of images of light and darkness in the Old Testament. How does John's use of light and darkness reflect Old Testament meanings? How is the dualism of light and darkness important for John's portrayal of Jesus' identity and mission?

Beginning With Moses and All the Prophets (45 minutes)

- Again, the week's readings portray Jesus causing controversy by what he says and does. Work through John 8–10, one chapter at a time, to see why Jesus' identity and mission generated so much controversy.

  John 8—Recall that Jesus' teachings in John 7–8 are set during Sukkoth (Booths). Refer to Leviticus 23:39-43 for the purpose of the festival. In the total group imagine what a Jewish pilgrim to the Feast of Booths in Jerusalem would have seen and heard. Then hear selected portions of Jesus' teaching read aloud: John 7:37-39; 8:12-13; 8:28-29; 8:31-32; 8:42-44; 8:56-58. What challenges to Jewish faith would a devout Jew at the festival have heard in Jesus' words? What role does the setting of these teachings—in the Temple—play in what Jesus says about his identity and mission?

  John 9—Begin by turning to **GC 26-G**. In groups of three or four discuss the themes of sight and blindness in the healing of the man born blind. Compare the four passages with these questions in mind: (1) Where is the story set? (2) What prompts Jesus to perform the healing? (3) How does Jesus accomplish the healing? (4) How do the blind in the stories respond to being healed? (5) Who besides the blind are present in the stories and how are they involved? After working through those questions in each group, discuss these additional questions: What do the unique features of John 9 say about Jesus' purpose in healing the man born blind and about John's purpose in telling the story? What connections does John's telling of the story make between sin and blindness? between healing and judgment? between religious tradition and divine authority? In what way is John 9:39-41 a commentary on the entire story of Jesus in John's Gospel?

John 10—Before turning to John 10, hear Ezekiel 34:1-16 read aloud. Then with the prophet's words in mind, discuss Jesus' teaching in John 10:1-18, 22-30. How do Jesus' words promise to fulfill Ezekiel's words? How do Jesus' words go beyond the prophet's words? Why does Jesus use shepherd imagery to speak of both his mission and his death? Now turn to **GC 26-1** and hear persons' observations comparing the accusations against Jesus. Conclude discussion with these questions: What do the accusations of being demon-possessed and a blasphemer say about Jesus and about his opponents at this point in John's Gospel? What do you think John intends his readers to understand by ending the narrative in Chapters 5–10 with 10:40-42?

Yet the World Did Not Know Him (45 minutes)

At least two elements are common to all of Jesus' controversies in John 8–10: "the Jews" and "the world." Referring to study manual pages 245–246 and daily notes, explore each element in groups of three or four.

- Compare Jesus' references to "the Jews" with references made by the narrator. First locate and read John 4:22; 13:33; 18:20, 36, making note of what is said. Repeat the process with John 5:16-18; 8:48, 52, 57; 9:22; 10:24, 31, 33. Then discuss these questions: What distinguishes Jesus' references to "the Jews" from the narrator's references? What impression of the Jews did you get from reading Jesus' references? from reading the narrator's references? What do you make of the fact that it is Jesus who speaks harsh words *to* the Jews, and John's narrator who says harsh words *about* the Jews? How does the observation that "Jesus never argues with anyone who is not a Jew" affect your understanding of John's portrayal of "the Jews"?
- Call attention to the quotation in large type on study manual page 246. Describe "the world" that did not know Jesus in John's day. Describe "the world" that does not know Jesus in our day. Read aloud John 3:16. What do you think it means to say this verse "is the great *nevertheless* that becomes the story of Jesus"?
- In John, Jesus' public mission is confrontational. In what way does the Jesus in John continue to confront "the world" in our day? On what does "the world" rely to discredit Jesus and his teachings? When do you as a disciple experience the Jesus in John as confrontational?

Do You Want to Become His Disciples, Too? (20 minutes)

- When have you found that understanding of Jesus' teachings in John has eluded you, causing you to "struggle along in his company"? What kept you from turning back?
- Read Psalm 23 in unison. How do you hear the voice of the Good Shepherd speaking to you? Where are you being led in your discipleship?
- In pairs respond to the question on study manual page 249, *Who is this Jesus that the world you know does not recognize or accept?*

Going Forth (10 minutes)

- Preview Lesson 27. Hear prayer concerns.
- Pray in unison the prayer on study manual page 249.
- View Video Segment 26 Part II

NOTES

Note: Locate emblems of discipleship (small crosses) in the enrollment kit for use in Session 30. Order more if necessary.

27 That They May Believe

Coming Together (30 minutes)

- Gather with prayer.
- Sing or read the words of a hymn.
  "Come, My Way, My Truth, My Life" or "Jesu, Jesu"
- Prepare to view video. Ask group members to open their Gospel Comparisons to **GC 27-1** to have it ready for use after viewing the video. **Presenter:** Carolyn A. Osiek, Professor of New Testament, Catholic Theological Union.
  Listen for the purposes of the anointings, for people's responses, for Jesus' response.
- View Video Segment 27 Part I.
- Discuss after viewing:
    Referring both to notes from watching the video and **GC 27-1**, discuss these questions: What responses to the anointings did you hear or read about? What do you make of the fact that we learn of Mary's motivation not from Mary but from Jesus? What common elements as well as differences did you notice in the four stories? What messages do the stories convey about Jesus?

Beginning With Moses and All the Prophets (45 minutes)

- In groups of three identify the several levels of meaning in the story of the raising of Lazarus. Consider the story in phases—John 11:1-16, 17-37, 38-44. Refer to daily notes on Scripture, observations from suggestions under Day 1, and "Jesus Confronts the Living and Summons the Dead" on study manual pages 254–257. What meaning is found in each phase of the story? Consider the levels of meaning for the persons involved in the story and for readers of the story. How might the meaning in the story be different for persons in the story and readers of the story?
- In the same groups of three, still concentrating on the story of Lazarus, identify the individuals and groups involved in the story and then look at the events through each person's and each group's eyes and experience of the event. What part did each person (or group) play in the story? How would each have viewed and understood the event? Then discuss these questions: Why is the raising of Lazarus considered Jesus' greatest sign? How do you account for the fact that people responded both with belief and rejection?
- In twos or threes consider Jesus' entry into Jerusalem. Use **GC 27-2** to guide discussion of Jesus' actions and the people's actions as reported in the four Gospel accounts. Also look up Zechariah 9:9-10. What differences did you see in the reports of those who went for the colt? Compare Jesus' response in John with the crowd's response in the Synoptics.

- In two groups examine Jesus' own summary of his mission using suggestions (1) through (3) under Day 5. Review the biblical passages for each theme. Then in the total group, on the basis of this summary, describe who Jesus was and what his mission was.

That They May Believe (45 minutes)

- Trace the recurring emphasis on the word *believe* and the action of believing. Work in groups of three or four. Begin with the commentary on study manual pages 254–259. Keep in mind the stories and accounts in John 11 and 12. Why do Jesus and John put such emphasis on the action *believe?* What does Jesus mean by *believe?*
- Examine two aspects of John's way of preparing readers for Jesus' death: "the hour" and glorification. Work in groups of three or four. Consult Scriptures and suggestions for Day 5, "A Reader's Guide to the Passion Story" on study manual pages 257–258, **GC 27-3**, and "'Glorification' in John" on study manual page 261. Again recall mentions of "hour" and "glorified" in John 11–12. Discuss this question: What does the study manual mean when it says "This Gospel does not make it easy for us to understand Jesus' view of his death?"
- Concentrate now on six of the main ideas in this lesson. Form pairs and assign one of the six quotations in large type to each pair. Instruct the pairs to talk about what the quotation is saying, to identify related Scripture and lesson material that support or explain the quotation, and to be prepared to say what the quotation means for understanding Jesus and for following Jesus. In the total group hear each pair's thoughts on the assigned quotation.
- One of the purposes for the suggestions of things to look for in each day's assignments is to help readers read for detail. Take some time to allow persons to talk about what they are learning by paying close attention to what the text says. Invite persons to work individually to identify one suggestion under each day's assignments that provided new insight into a particular passage or verse, that surprised or even shocked, that made a point that was completely new to the person. Allow time for persons to scan each day's suggestions and to choose one suggestion to talk about. Then in two groups work through the five days one day at a time hearing each person say what suggestion had been particularly enlightening.

Do You Want to Become His Disciples, Too? (20 minutes)

- Comment that in John's Gospel whoever believes in Jesus also believes what he says about himself and his mission. Work in two groups to identify all the statements Jesus made about himself in John 11–12.
- In groups of three hear one another's written responses to the questions on study manual page 260, *Who is this Jesus you believe in? How does what you believe conform to what Jesus says about himself?*

Going Forth (10 minutes)

- Preview Lesson 28. Hear prayer concerns.
- Pray in unison the prayer on study manual page 260.
- View Video Segment 27 Part II.

28 Jesus' Legacy

Coming Together (30 minutes)

- Gather with prayer.
- Sing or read the words to a hymn.
  "To God Be the Glory" or "O Church of God, United"
- Prepare to view video.
  Presenter: Craig R. Koester, Professor of New Testament, Luther Seminary. Listen for what Jesus means by the term *glorify* and how it summarizes his ministry on earth.
- View Video Segment 28 Part I.
- Discuss after viewing:
  In what ways do Jesus' signs in John reveal God's glory? What does it mean to say that "in John's Gospel the Crucifixion is the central act of glorification"? How is the coming of the Spirit related to Jesus' glorious works of power on earth and his return to heavenly glory?

Beginning With Moses and All the Prophets (60 minutes)

- In John 13–17 what Jesus says and does during his last meal with the disciples is key to understanding his legacy. With that in mind examine these five chapters in three parts.
  The footwashing—Consider the distinctiveness of the Last Supper in John 13 in comparison to Luke 22:1-34. In the total group work through both Gospel accounts answering these questions about each one: (1) How does the narrator set the scene? (2) What does Jesus do at the table? (3) How does Jesus interpret what he does? (4) What command and promise does Jesus give his disciples? Now imagine yourself as one of the disciples, first around the table in Luke's account, and then around the table in John's account. As individuals, spend a minute or two in each scene. Imagine what you see, smell, hear, taste, and feel. Imagine how you react to what Jesus is doing and saying. Then in pairs or threes talk about your impressions of Jesus at the table in John as compared to Jesus at the table in Luke. Identify differences and similarities. Use these questions to guide discussion: What does John's emphasis on the footwashing rather than on the meal say about John's view of Jesus' mission? of the disciple's mission? What does the love command (John 13:34) coming for the first time in this context say about the meaning of the last meal in John? What message about discipleship does John convey in the way he portrays Peter and Judas in Chapter 13?
  The farewell discourse—Explore these three chapters one at a time. (1) In John 14 Jesus responds to requests from three of his disciples, Thomas (14:5); Philip (14:8), and Judas (14:22). Assign one of the requests to each of three groups with this task: Identify what the disciple wanted to know and summarize Jesus' response. Then in the total group

discuss these questions: What do the disciples' requests reveal about their understanding of who Jesus is. How does John's arrangement of these teachings as direct responses to disciples' requests help us understand what Jesus means? How would you characterize the believer's relation to Jesus according to John 14?

(2) The image of the vine in John 15 conveys both positive and negative images. Recall the vine imagery in the Old Testament Scriptures for Day 3 and discuss how Jesus' message in the vine metaphor includes and expands upon the meanings of those Scriptures. How do love, joy, and obedience intertwine to produce the fruit of discipleship?

(3) Recall Jesus' teachings about the Spirit in John 16 and review study manual pages 268–270. How would you describe the relation of the Spirit to the life of the believer, to the world, and to Jesus? What understanding of the Spirit is necessary in order to avoid making the Spirit a substitute for Jesus?

Jesus' prayer—One of the themes in this week's readings in John, especially Jesus' prayer in Chapter 17, is *unity*. Form three groups to compare Paul's concern for unity with Jesus' prayer for unity: Group 1 (Romans 8:28-39), Group 2 (Ephesians 4:1-16), Group 3 (Philippians 2:1-13). How does the church's mission benefit from unity among believers—according to Jesus? according to Paul?

Jesus' Legacy (30 minutes)

- In John 13-17, Jesus makes clear the nature of his legacy through (1) a symbolic action–footwashing; (2) a vivid image—vine; and (3) the promise of continued companionship—Spirit. In pairs or threes describe what Jesus bequeaths to his disciples—then and now—by his action, his image, and his promise.
- Consider the implications of the use of "abide" in John 15 and 1 John (NRSV). Hear John 15:4-7 and then 1 John 4:7-15 read aloud. Call attention to the statement on study manual page 270 that the idea of abiding means remaining not sojourning. How would you describe the kind of discipleship the word "abide" suggests? What do you think is the greatest hindrance to "abiding" discipleship in our day?
- Jesus' legacy imparts love (13:34), peace (14:27), and joy (15:11). According to John 13–17, what is required of believers to receive any of the three?

Do You Want to Become His Disciples, Too? (20 minutes)

- Talk with a partner about what factors make it difficult for you to love fellow believers, especially members of your church family.
- Hear written responses called for under "Jesus' Farewell" on study manual page 273.
- Then in the same pairs hear responses to the question on study manual page 272, *What have you learned about Jesus that you want to pass on to others?*

Going Forth (10 minutes)

- Preview Lesson 29. Hear prayer concerns.
- Pray in unison the prayer on study manual page 272.
- View Video Segment 28 Part II.

29 Mission Completed

Coming Together (30 minutes)

- Gather with prayer.
- Sing or read the words of a hymn.
  "Lift High the Cross" or "O Love Divine, What Hast Thou Done"
- Prepare to view video.
  Presenter: Joel B. Green, Dean of Academic Affairs and Professor of New Testament Interpretation, Asbury Theological Seminary.
  Listen for three reasons the question, Why did Jesus have to die? demands attention and for three Gospel affirmations of why Jesus had to die.
- View Video Segment 29 Part 1.
- Discuss after viewing:
  What are some reasons persons might ask the question, Why did Jesus have to die? What is the larger context that gives the cross its significance? How do the Gospels make clear that Jesus' death on the cross was the working out of God's purpose of saving the world? In what way does Jesus' death serve as a model for disciples?

Beginning With Moses and All the Prophets (60 minutes)

- Follow the account in John 18–20 of the way Jesus completed his mission. Work through the five days of assignments one day at a time. Follow the story in John and see how other assigned Scriptures illuminate the story. Identify differences and similarities in the accounts of John and Luke. Look for features that give the Gospel of John its distinctive character. Work in groups of three or four. Vary the makeup of the groups by asking one person in each group to move to another group each time the work moves to the next day's assignment.
  Day 1—Follow the events in John 18:1-27 as they unfold. What took place? Hear what persons noted and observed in responding to suggestions (1) through (3) under Day 1 and what they discovered in using **GC 29-1** by following suggestions (4) and (5) under Day 1.
  Day 2—Follow the action in John 18:28–19:16. Refer to study manual commentary about Jesus and Pilate beginning in the last paragraph on study manual page 279 and continuing on page 280. What sense do you have of Jesus and of Pilate in this account? What is the meaning running under the words and actions in this account but not apparent in what is happening? Hear what persons noted and observed in responding to suggestions (1), (2), (4), and (5) under Day 2 and what they discovered in using **GC 29-2** by following suggestion (3) under Day 2.
  Day 3—Follow the events in John 19:17-30. What do other assigned passages contribute to understanding the event John reports? Hear what persons noted and observed in responding to suggestions (1), (3), (4),

and (5) under Day 3 and what differences and similarities they discovered in comparing the two accounts in **GC 29-3**.

Day 4—Follow the account in John 19:31-42 giving particular attention to the day and the people talked about in the passage. Indicate how each of the Old Testament passages relates to what John reports. Hear what persons noted in responding to suggestions (1) and (2) under Day 4 and what they discovered in following the instructions for **GC 29-4**. Hear how persons describe the tone of the three accounts.

Day 5—Follow the events in John 20 paying particular attention to the actions and reactions of the people in the account. What feelings or emotions come through the story? How are the emotions related to what the people discover and experience? Hear what persons noted and observed in responding to suggestions (1), (2), and (4) through (6).

Mission Completed (30 minutes)

■ Introduce the idea of the glorification of Jesus by asking the group to read aloud the quotation in large print on study manual page 280. Then read John 12:23-24; 13:31-32; 17:1, 5. Scan the surrounding verses to get some understanding of what is meant by glorification. Recall what you heard about glorification in the video from the previous session. Then discuss this question: Why does John emphasize Jesus' glorification rather than his suffering?

■ Begin consideration of Jesus' final words in John by reading and comparing Jesus' last words in the four Gospels printed in **GC 29-G**. How do Jesus' final words in John express the distinctive character of John's Gospel? Now in groups of three or four review "It Is Finished" on study manual pages 280–281 to understand the breadth of meaning in Jesus' last words in John. Identify four instances where those words point back across John's whole Gospel. Discuss this question: What message do you take from Jesus' words, "It is finished"?

■ In the total group review "So That the Scriptures Might Be Fulfilled" on study manual pages 281–282 and respond to this point: "The fulfillment of Scripture means that God's word has been kept in Jesus and his mission." What is the meaning in that statement?

Do You Want to Become His Disciples, Too? (20 minutes)

■ Hear "They Have No Wine" read aloud. Discuss this question: How do you make sense of Jesus' innocent suffering?

■ In groups of three or four hear responses to the question on study manual page 283, *In what sense are you a beneficiary of who Jesus is and what he did, and what difference does that make in your living?*

Going Forth (10 minutes)

■ Preview Lesson 30. Hear prayer concerns.
■ Pray in unison the prayer on study manual page 283.
■ View Video Segment 29 Part II.

Note to the leader: Call attention to the considerable amount of reading and writing required in preparation for Session 30. Ask the group to write out their selected passages to read. Make plans for closing worship that includes a meal and Holy Communion. Emphasize that Session 30 will take longer than two-and-a-half hours.

30 Looking Back at Jesus' Future

Preparing for Session 30

To see that Lesson 30 calls for a different kind of daily preparation by group members, turn to study manual page 284 and scan the paragraphs under "This Time: Beginning With John 21," and glance at the daily assignments. Similarly, the weekly session calls for a different approach, schedule, and sequence of activity as explained here.

The Session

- The weekly session begins with a look back at all four Gospels, then narrows the focus to John 21 and the lesson's commentary, and concludes with worship.
- Participants will have read all four Gospels and chosen up to six passages from each Gospel that express for them what each Gospel wants to say about Jesus. Session procedure calls for hearing all persons read the passages they selected and say why they chose them—one Gospel at a time.
- A second time of unhurried listening involves persons' written responses to the question at the end of the lesson, *Who is the Jesus you take with you from this study?*
- Notice that no time allotments are indicated for the different activities in this session. Nearly all conversation takes place in the total group so allow plenty of time to listen to one another, time for each person to talk and others to listen.

The Worship

- A service of worship that incorporates eating a simple meal, viewing the video segment, and celebrating Holy Communion closes the session and the thirty-week study of JESUS IN THE GOSPELS. Preview the worship service on study manual pages 292–295 to assign readers and to be aware of materials needed, such as hymnals.

The Preparation

- Consider an outdoor setting—in a park, by the lake, at the seashore for an unhurried time (more than two-and-a-half hours) of reflection, conversation, and listening.
- Plan the meal—bread, cheese, grains, fruit, beverage or—in the spirit of the story—fish from a grill and bread. Seating for the meal should allow for conversation or silence.
- Gather the materials for the worship setting—a table with a white cloth, a tall white candle, matches, sand (available from most hardware stores), and small crosses (check to be sure enough crosses—one for

each person in the group—have been ordered and received).

- Prepare for viewing the video—Video Segment 30 includes only words, art, and music, no presentation by a scholar. The video requires no introduction and no discussion follows. Set up the equipment (for VHS or DVD) and cue the video so it can be turned on and off at the appropriate time during worship.
- Arrange for Holy Communion—Follow the practice of your denomination in securing, preparing, and consecrating the elements for Holy Communion.

Looking Back at Jesus' Future

Coming Together

- Pray in unison the prayer on study manual page 291.
- Sing or read the words of a hymn.
  "Take My Life, and Let It Be" or Stanzas 1 and 2 of "Forth in Thy Name, O Lord"

Looking Back at the Gospels

- Hear each person in turn read the passages chosen from each Gospel that express what the Gospel wants the reader to understand about Jesus, that express the characteristic or distinctive emphasis of each Gospel as a whole and say why the particular passages were chosen. Though daily assignments (Scriptures for Days 2–5) are not in canonical order, start with Matthew and work through the Gospels one at a time in sequence. Follow this procedure: The first person will read up to six passages chosen from Matthew and explain why they were chosen. Each person in turn will do the same until all persons have read and spoken about the passages chosen from Matthew. Then discuss these questions: How does the Gospel of Matthew end by looking forward? How does the end of Matthew's Gospel reflect what led up to it? Repeat the process for hearing persons' chosen passages from Mark, from Luke, and from John. Adapt and discuss the same two questions for use with Mark, with Luke, and with John.

Looking Now at John 21

- As background for studying John 21, look together at the purpose of the Gospel of John according to John 20:30-31. Hear it read aloud. Then hear the purpose of John 21 read aloud from John 21:1. According to John 21:14, the occasion reported in this chapter was Jesus' third post-Resurrection appearance to his disciples. Look up and read reports of the two previous appearances—John 20:19-23, 26-29.
- Look at John 21, focusing on the people in the account—those who are named but silent and those who speak and act. Form two groups and instruct the groups to read John 21 silently, concentrating on the people who were there, on what was going on, and on the interactions among the people. Then respond to these questions one at a time: What images and recollections do you have from past study of the people present that morning on the beach? What words or actions of Jesus call up earlier events or images? Now follow Jesus and Simon Peter through the events in this chapter as the story progresses. What do you

see and hear in actions and exchanges? What sense do you have of what is going on between the two of them? We get some idea of how Simon was feeling as Jesus questioned him, but what do you imagine others were thinking and feeling as they heard the exchange between Jesus and Simon Peter? The only other person to speak in this story is the "disciple whom Jesus loved." Hear what persons discovered about this unnamed disciple when they looked up references for suggestions (4), (5), and (6) under Day 1. What, if anything, do you make of the fact that it was the "disciple whom Jesus loved," rather than Simon Peter who recognized the man on the beach as "the Lord"? In what sense were the disciples aware that the Jesus who served them breakfast was the same Jesus they had known and yet no longer the same?

The Lord's Breakfast

- Recall in the total group the events and conversation at the previous meal Jesus hosted (John 13) and the events that took place between that supper and this breakfast. What has changed for those who are at the breakfast on the beach? Now consider the four episodes in this chapter, one episode at a time: John 21:2-8, 9-14, 15-19, 20-23. Follow this process: For each episode hear the related verses read aloud and then, drawing on information from study manual pages 288–289, discuss this question: What does this episode show about the resurrected Jesus that is important for the disciples in the future? for today's disciples in the future? Repeat the process for each episode. After considering all four episodes respond to this question: What is the message to you in this statement: "When the resurrected Jesus exited the tomb, he entered the future as its Lord"?
- Think together about the idea that in this breakfast on the beach the risen, glorified Jesus shows himself in the ordinary. Explain to one another what "ordinary" means here. Then invite persons to tell of personal experiences of meeting Jesus in the "ordinary."

Do You Want to Become His Disciples, Too?

- Invite the group to read together John 21:22 from study manual page 284. Comment that Jesus' call to follow expects an answer and leaves no room for negotiating. Then discuss these questions: How do we try to negotiate? What issues do we raise to which Jesus might respond, "What is that to you . . . ?"
- Now, in the total group, hear each person's written response to the question on study manual page 290, *Who is the Jesus you take with you from this study?* Allow time for persons to talk about how they answered a similar question at the beginning of the study and how their perception and understanding of Jesus has changed through the thirty weeks of study.

Invitation to Worship

- A time of worship, using the order of service on study manual pages 292–295, concludes this session and this study of JESUS IN THE GOSPELS.
- Take a brief break and set up for the worship and meal.

JESUS IN THE GOSPELS Group Members

Name _____ Address _____

Phone _____ _____

Name _____ Address _____

Phone _____ _____

Name _____ Address _____

Phone _____ _____

Name _____ Address _____

Phone _____ _____

Name _____ Address _____

Phone _____ _____

Name _____ Address _____

Phone _____ _____

Name _____ Address _____

Phone _____ _____

Name _____ Address _____

Phone _____ _____

Name _____ Address _____

Phone _____ _____

Name _____ Address _____

Phone _____ _____

Name _____ Address _____

Phone _____ _____

Name _____ Address _____

Phone _____ _____

Notes

CPSIA information can be obtained at www.ICGtesting.com
Printed in the USA
LVOW09s1048020514

384014LV00001B/4/P